BUILL

YOUR

DREAM

LIFE

How Property Can Help You Quit the Rat Race

BRONWEN VEARNCOMBE

Building Your Dream Life

First published in 2020 by

Panoma Press Ltd
48 St Vincent Drive, St Albans, Herts, AL1 5SJ, UK
info@panomapress.com
www.panomapress.com

Book layout by Neil Coe.

978-1-784529-06-2

The right of Bronwen Vearncombe to be identified as the author of this work has been asserted in accordance with sections 77 and 78 of the Copyright, Designs and Patents Act 1988.

A CIP catalogue record for this book is available from the British Library.

Testimonials

'Clear concise and directive content that will inspire. An excellent guidebook!'

Tracy Plaice, Director, Visual Solutions Ltd

'Really accessible for someone who doesn't know anything about property investing.'

Lyndy Geddes, Director, Pink Personal Training

Acknowledgements

Our achievements have been the culmination of so much learning from people who have given their time freely and inspired us to persevere.

I'd like to specifically thank all those fellow property investors who helped encourage us at the start, taught us along the way – both formally and informally – and continue to support us as we learn new strategies and adapt our business. In particular, those in the property investors network (pin).

Disclaimer

Case studies: All the numbers were correct at the time of purchase. Costs such as stamp duty and mortgage payments will change with policy and interest rates. Always check your personal tax position and purchase costs before buying.

Foreword

Like many people, Bronwen Vearncombe dreamed of leaving the corporate rat race and having more time to spend with her family and travel the world. Unlike many people, Bronwen actually took action and achieved her dream through property investment in just 12 months.

I met Bronwen as a beginner, when she decided to invest in her education and she and her husband, John, became top performers on my Property Mastermind Programme in 2014. I was impressed by Bronwen's dedication and commitment. As she and John built a very profitable property portfolio, people began to seek Bronwen's advice and I know that she is very generous in sharing her knowledge and experience with others, through her Property Investing Foundation.

Reading the newspapers, in the context of some startling regulatory changes in recent years, people are put off property investing because they worry it is no longer profitable. Bronwen is proof that if you genuinely understand the sector, there are always opportunities.

In her book, Bronwen shares her fascinating story, explaining what worked, what didn't work so well and how she overcame challenges along the way. The book tackles mindset, team-building and the essentials you need to know to be successful, including detailed case studies.

Investing in property is a bit like having a baby. There's never a 'right' time. Bronwen's story is an inspiration to the millions who feel stuck in the rat race but long for a more fulfilling life. Her book gives readers a great overview of what they need to succeed in property investing, in the hope that they too will be inspired to take action.

Invest with knowledge, invest with skill.

Simon Zutshi

Author of the international best seller *Property Magic*
Founder, property investors network

Contents

Introduction:
Planning Permission

Want to earn money while you sleep? Perhaps by investing in property? Whether you're a complete beginner scared of taking your first step, or a mature investor looking to expand your portfolio and take your earnings to the next level, wouldn't it be great to have a book that tells you everything you need to know?

That's where I started in 2014, and in this book you are going to hear my story from the office to the wide open ocean. The highs, the lows, lessons, emotions, real case studies and top tips learned along the way. It's not been easy but it's been worth the hard work. It's so exciting to know that it's possible to get that precious time back into your life and to have choices again. So let's begin…

Our Old Lives as Corporate Drones

"Instead of wondering when your next vacation is, maybe you should set up a life you don't need to escape from." Seth Godin

As I slumped into my seat on the morning commuter train, panting with the effort of running to the far end of the platform to get a seat, I couldn't help but think there must be more to life than this. I looked around at the tired faces of the people around me – many in their 50s and 60s – and thought I don't want to be like them at that age. But with the state of my Lloyds Bank pension at that time, how could I make sure that I wouldn't be just like them when I reached their age? It was time to find a way out of the rat race.

Looking back, I laugh at the things I did just to secure a seat on the train before they were all taken. Getting to the platform to stand just where the doors opened before the train arrived; on the way home racing down the train platform ahead of others. I remember regularly sitting on the carriage floor on a hot day after running for the train. Stress, stress, stress. At the time I accepted that this was what everyone did to earn a good living, wasn't it? My health suffered too, as I'd often pick up the viruses from the coughs and splutters around me in the packed train carriage. I wanted to scream out "Blow your nose!" to the guy opposite who thought it OK to sniff all the way to Waterloo. Oh, and the guilt I felt if I didn't get my laptop out to complete that piece of work I'd left unfinished when I'd escaped the office earlier.

Why did no one talk to each other on the commuter trains? We were the same people, same carriage, stuck in our ways, heads in the newspapers and the clouds, rarely a nod to each other. Ah, but when there was a problem – signal fault at Basingstoke, leaves on the line, too much white stuff when it dusted with snow, or sadly a jumper at Clapham Junction – heaven forbid we'd be late for our team meeting! Then we'd chat and commiserate with each other. It's funny looking at what 'normal' was back then.

The only day I used to look forward to was Saturday, because Sunday became the day before the rat race again. I'd start to get that 'back-to-school' feeling I remembered from when I was a child. I'd been working for Lloyds Bank in various guises for over 20 years and enjoyed the roles and responsibilities. But it was hard work. Holidays were a great release, but I'd only ever get two consecutive weeks once a year and only 30 days in total. It didn't seem like much.

With a loving husband, John, two children, Robert and Laura, and an elderly mother, my life was pretty full. Robert was 19 going on 20 and had settled in at university, so had effectively left home. Laura was 17 and at college studying for her A levels, on the daily bus to and fro, playing music loudly in her room, and immersing herself in social media. Both my mother and mother-in-law were in their 80s and whilst fit and healthy at that time, we knew that there could be health issues looming on the horizon. But how could we find more time to enjoy their company in the precious years we had left with them?

Work/life balance was often talked about in my career, yet my feelings were always that I wanted more of the 'life' bit. When the chance came during a big restructure of the bank, I took it, though the process took over nine months.

John had dabbled in a number of jobs, all focused mainly on helping large retailers or manufacturers with their information technology processes and systems thinking. As a consultant during this time, he was also commuting and working hard to fulfil someone else's strategy. Our careers had dovetailed well so that one of us was around for the children when needed, but our time together was pretty limited. We'd often talk about perhaps working abroad, maybe taking control as contractors in the future to allow us more choice.

Escaping the rat race with just one property

Well, I'd not been hanging about doing nothing during those nine months before leaving the bank. I was considering a job closer to home and in an area that really interested me, the National Health Service. Private to public sector was quite a transition, but a rewarding one in the early days. It still didn't quite give me the 'life' I was dreaming about, but I was at least more in control of my days and was a touch closer to home (with the exception of a 12-month stint on the Isle of Wight!).

The catalyst happened in the form of considering our savings and investments. With so many bank shares I'd collected over the years, and their plummeting value during the recession, I decided to sell them and invest the money in something that would provide a higher return. Let's try property, we thought. It's getting a lot of press and we love our commuting city of Winchester, so let's find a flat to rent out, using the share funds plus some savings as a deposit. With very little hesitation, John and I bought a two-bed ex-council flat right in the heart of the city and, as the agent had promised, we let it immediately.

So now, what did we know about property? Very little. It's important to me to be very aware of rules and regulations; I suppose that's the banking education I'd had. Suddenly being classed as a 'landlord', I thought I needed to know the rules. Two 'recommended on Amazon' books later and with one in particular resonating with us both, we came to a huge realisation. Perhaps property investing could bring us more than just a bit of spare cash and some capital growth. Maybe, just maybe, we could reduce the hours we worked and replace some of our corporate income.

"It's never going to work in the south," I said as we thought about the theory we'd read about. The house prices were far too expensive to be able to get the returns that were quoted in the book. So we went along to a few property networking meetings, vowing not to be 'sold to' and trying to sit at the back. We did a lot of checking of courses and trainers and eventually signed up to do a three-day course to really understand our current responsibilities as landlords and the possibilities of doing more.

After the three-day course with the property investors network (pin), we felt like we wanted to invest in more in-depth training. Our choice of education provider was born out of trust and values that were aligned with ours. We were also attracted by the style of learning, the accountability and support provided and the fact that classroom learning was once a month on a weekend.

Speaking at first hand with people who had learned from the founder Simon Zutshi, and doing our own research too, meant that we felt confident to part with a large amount of money and commit to this venture. Whilst daunted and pretty fearful of the commitment we had made, we both also felt that if we were to spend money on such a structured course over a whole year we *had* to make it work! I'll never forget the responsibility we both felt, but at least we were doing it together so we could share the burden.

As for our family and loved ones, we'd talked to them all about our plans to invest in property, which of course is hard to explain easily without it seeming massively risky! We didn't say how much it was costing to do the training, but they seemed supportive on the whole.

It was around this time that my mother's health deteriorated. After a short spell in hospital she'd gone into a care home just a mile away to rehabilitate before going home. Just weeks after, she passed away and joined my father on the most appropriate day possible – Valentine's Day. With John's mother having been diagnosed with a brain tumour and passing away the previous year, they were both a reason for us to create more time in our lives and now they were gone. We both found ourselves as orphans and we were determined to be successful in their memories.

Alongside around 60 people on the Property Mastermind Programme, we followed the process over the ten months of the course. We worked very hard, built a portfolio of multi-let houses for young professionals, and started a conversion of a house into six flats. We ended the programme as one of the chosen top five performers for the year. I am so proud of that and remember vividly the day we had to stand on the stage (shaking like leaves in the wind) and present to our colleagues about what we had achieved, giving specific details of each property deal. This event was filmed live and I asked Robert and Laura to try to watch it live too, as I wanted them to understand why we were just so busy that year and somewhat distracted from family life.

The actual recording of this is on my website and I know it inspires others even now. You can find it here: http://bit.ly/AboutBV. I do admit to having shed a few tears for my mother, who would have been the first person I'd told when the winners were announced. She'd have been so proud.

Within a few months, John had handed in his notice at work and I reduced my hours down to three days a week so we could continue to grow the portfolio. The following year, I left my corporate job too. This was the scariest thing of all – sacrificing my monthly salary and seeing the payslip in my hand every month no matter what. Was this really the right decision? What if? Fear crept in. I told myself I could always go back and get another job (secretly determined to make sure I didn't). We'd come this far; surely with more time in our days and not having to juggle life with our corporate jobs, we could make it work. Still, it was Christmas time, so I could forget a lot of it while I had more time with family. I felt euphoric at times, then more thoughtful...

A new year started, and with it our new life as full-time property investors. The hard work continued in earnest. We were excited and had clear goals for the coming year. We continued with our learning and joined a graduate group so we could still have support. This helped us focus. We were asked to host a monthly property networking group in Southampton and then to lead a local Mastermind learning group each month too. We both enjoyed helping others learn and providing support from our experience.

Two years later, we found ourselves living our dreams and turning our dream board into reality. John signed up for the Clipper Round the World yacht race – racing across the world's oceans – and I followed him by plane, taking part in my own adventures and dream experiences along the way. I even set up my own property investing online training and coached people too. We were away from the UK for a year while our property business continued to provide us with the income needed.

In this book, I'm sharing five key areas that helped with our success, the learnings and top tips that made a difference, and not just the essential tasks, but also the mindset shifts that were necessary along the way. There are detailed case studies of our deals to bring things to life. I'll share the excitement of being able to follow our dreams and travel the world too. It's definitely not been easy, and of course there are ups and downs along the way, but I'm going to bring you the reality of things that can go wrong, the lessons learned, and some tricks that work if you want to do something similar. It really is possible to invest in property and achieve an income to give you time back in your life. No matter how small or big your aims are, the process is the same.

CHAPTER 1:

CONSTRUCTING THE FOUNDATIONS

STEP 1.
Learn and Plan

"Goals. There's no telling what you can do when you get inspired by them. There's no telling what you can do when you believe in them; and there's no telling what will happen when you act upon them."

Jim Rohn

With any new venture it can seem daunting and impossible. In this section I'm going to share with you some of the very basics: how we started with our planning and setting goals to aim at. Many people will try to learn for free and listen to the negativity that friends and colleagues express and then make excuses not to continue. We were inspired by people who were successful and actively investing and wanted to emulate that. Here's how we set about it.

1.1 How Does Property Investing Work?

Basically, property investing is the provision of a rental home for a tenant, with a contract in place, and the rental income less the costs provides a profit and income to the owner (landlord). It can also apply to those that might purchase a property, refurbish it and then sell it for a profit, sometimes known as a 'flip'. (That's quite a different business and not a strategy I've worked with as my aim is to buy and hold for cash flow.)

The traditional funding route is through property loans (mortgages) and if you're purchasing any buy-to-let or investment property there are special types of lending products. These work just like the mortgage on your own home, but have other considerations if you are letting the property, such as the rent cover needed on the specific deal. A mortgage is a loan taken out to buy property or land. Most run for 25 years but the term can be shorter or longer. The loan is 'secured' against the value of the property until it's paid off. If you can't keep up your repayments, the lender can repossess and sell it so they get their money back. The interest rates are directly related to the bank base rates.

Traditionally, a lender will loan 75% of the value of the property, leaving you with 25% to fund yourself (known as the deposit). The repayment can be the interest and capital together or interest only. The choices here depend on the investment strategy you are focusing on and professional advice is always recommended. The important thing here is your level of risk appetite and the cost of borrowing the funds. A mortgage is pretty much the cheapest way to borrow against a property, and with base rates the lowest they've been for over 40 years, it can be a sensible option. Of course everyone has a different level of risk appetite, so it's a personal decision on how much debt to have as a percentage of the value (also known as loan to value – LTV – or gearing). Given the economics of rental properties, the banks are keen to lend, but do have parameters to check against the rental income to assess how much they will lend.

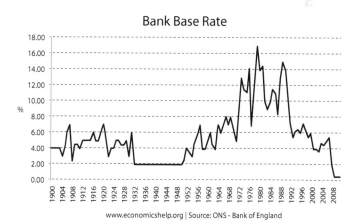

Bank Base Rate

www.economicshelp.org | Source: ONS - Bank of England

How we went about creating our initial seed capital was through remortgaging our home to release the equity that had built up over ten years. This was possible because UK house values tend to rise over a long period of time, so the lender was prepared to provide an additional lump sum advance against this increase. Of course you must always make sure that you can afford the monthly repayments and it is much easier to borrow when you have a good income in a corporate job. Using this equity money, we were able to invest in deposits for our buy-to-let investments, refurbishment costs, and generally chose to borrow on an interest-only basis to maximise our monthly profit.

So not only is UK property a good asset to borrow from, but the value of that asset tends to grow in the longer term too – capital growth. There are short-term blips in this because of economic and political situations, and also location, but the UK is an island with a growing population and we are not building enough new homes to meet anything like the demand. Affordability for first-time buyers is harder than it's ever been, as banks have tightened up on lending since the last recession, so there is a high demand for people needing to rent their own home, often well into their mid-30s and 40s.

You only need to look back at the property your grandparents or parents bought back in the 1970s or 1980s to understand how much the values have increased during one or two generations.

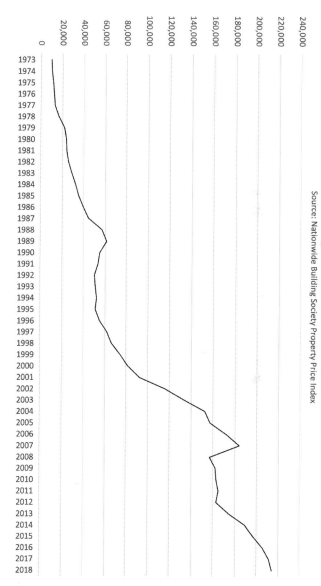

UK Avg House Prices Since 1973

Source: Nationwide Building Society Property Price Index

It's interesting to also see that even during the recession in 2008, which saw a big adjustment in prices, the increase has continued to rise above the pre-recession rate. The next graph illustrates that clearly. Of course this varies by geographical area in the UK with the south of England seeing the biggest recovery.

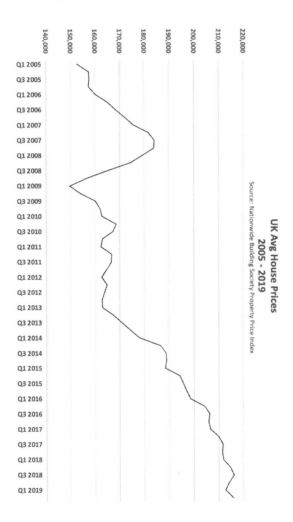

UK Avg House Prices 2005 - 2019

Source: Nationwide Building Society Property Price Index

The great thing about UK rental property is that it can provide a regular monthly cash flow after costs, and the overall value of the property will tend to rise over the long term too. The economics are clear and because demand to rent is high, then the rental income is high. As long as the costs are managed, the profit can provide a regular income.

It's easy to become an 'accidental' landlord when you perhaps move in with a partner and rather than sell your home you decide to rent it out. This is also the case when perhaps you decide to buy a holiday home and then let it while you are not using it. The economics are the same.

1.2 The Reason Why

Setting up from the start with a compelling reason provides real focus. In times of trouble and angst, returning to this reason helped motivate and drive us to continue. Our 'reason why' centred around the need to have more time to spend with our elderly mothers and our children. We had also long dreamed of having some quite specific travel adventures. My reasons were not necessarily the same as John's – in fact, they were quite different. We are our own people with different ideas. I actually found it pretty hard until some examples were given. I looked at what I am really passionate about and things I used to really enjoy when I was younger – wildlife and conservation.

We both wrote down our reasons in an affirmation letter to use later in the year. I even created a picture background on my mobile phone of the Namibian wildlife sanctuary,

Naankuse, that I wanted to volunteer at. That made it really visual for me.

Halfway through the year – so five months in – we opened our affirmation letters and reread what we had written about our reasons why. We read each other's and were spurred on to continue the hard work and to achieve our aims. Even now I still have Naankuse as the background on my phone. It continues to be my motivator now and reminds me that I can return for a few months each year to help with something I really love and believe makes a big difference – animal research. For John, his aim was to do more sailing and perhaps to cross an ocean, to travel and experience the culture of new countries. In fact, he wanted to support the wildlife sanctuary too. So much to inspire us both!

How to go about this yourself: Get thinking and drill down as much as you can to make the reason as specific as possible, and as real as possible. A technique I use with my coaching clients is to keep asking them "So what…?" or "So what will that give you?" Writing it down makes it feel real and helps focus the mind too.

How about an example: A common reason why is to have more time, to have freedom in one's life, to be financially free. To which I ask "So what will you choose to do with that time, freedom or money?" Another way to trigger this is to consider "If money wasn't an issue, what would you choose to do with your time?" You know when you've started to hit the spot when you get excited and enthusiastic. I hear it in my clients' voices and see it in their eyes.

Depending on how you like to be reminded, you might create a dream board of pictures of the things you've described – the events, the adventures, the feelings, the place, etc. The creativity will be helpful in the process, I assure you.

1.3 Goal Setting

Just as in my corporate days, I thought it critical to set goals to aim for. These needed to be realistic but also stretching. Five years is best as a longer-term goal and then work backwards to be very specific – say about Year 1. That way, you will have the confidence that you are moving in the right direction. For me, ten years was too far out to consider a possibility in my mind.

We set a first year goal at £2m worth of property and £60,000 pa gross income (£5,000 pm) – plenty to be able to leave our corporate jobs, but a massive stretch in our eyes at the time. I found it hard to look beyond that, but both of us leaving our corporate jobs was a big enough goal for me. We then determined the best strategy to give us this cash flow we needed and the average gross profit that strategy might bring per property. We picked one of the harder strategies – houses of multiple occupation (HMO) or multi-lets.

For some people, the corporate-style goal setting hasn't featured in their experience before. If this is the case, I'd be making the goals more focused on the very short-term end of the scale – monthly, weekly and daily. Your focus then becomes "What am I doing today to reach my weekly

⌣ ıl?" Derek Mills has a different approach along these lines, which he shares in his book *The 10-Second Philosophy*. He advocates setting your own standards to live by each and every day. By working on and achieving these daily standards you can easily reach and feel good about that.

1.4 Books to Read

There are several books we were advised to read before starting our property course and some of them were excellent. Here's a list of those I particularly enjoyed and a few others that I recommend. Everyone is different and only you know your true self, where you thrive and when you struggle. Consider which ones resonate with you and get reading.

Property Magic by **Simon Zutshi**

This book started our thinking and gave us insights into strategies that we had never heard of before. Using other people's money seemed to be very simplistic, but the case studies brought it to life and helped make sense of the reality. This is a book I give away with my learning programme as it's the fundamental guide that I used to build my own portfolio.

Think and Grow Rich by **Napoleon Hill**

This is a classic for anyone who wants to achieve more in their life as a whole. Although the book was written in 1937 and some of the language seems rather old, the concepts are still as valid as ever. It takes you through lots of examples in US corporations and real-life situations that make you think differently.

Rich Dad Poor Dad by **Robert Kiyosaki**

This book is about the author's personal story and helps you distinguish between assets and liabilities, understanding cash flow and the importance of investing and entrepreneurship in taking control of your financial future.

The 10-Second Philosophy by **Derek Mills**

This book supports the setting of shorter-term goals or 'standards', as Derek calls them. He encourages us to use words, phrases and questions we encounter in our everyday lives to stop, go inside and access our 'True Self'. This book is good for people who struggle with using 'goals' to drive their performance.

The Restless Executive by **Jo Simpson**

Don't be fooled by the title – this is not just for executives. It's for anyone who wants to discover their core values, their drivers and what motivates them. It is written as a story, and I gained a lot of insight into myself when I read this book.

Eat That Frog! by **Brian Tracy**

This book will help you get the most important things done. Brian Tracy is a prolific author of success books, and this is a great one to start with. We all have too much to do, and this book will help you focus on the right things first.

The Compound Effect by **Darren Hardy**

Another fantastic book, which explains how the small things we do consistently each day can have a huge impact on our future. This is a great philosophy, which is also very appropriate for property investing.

Take the Stairs by **Rory Vaden**

I love this book, which helps you understand the importance of doing the things that you know you should do but don't really want to do. It is packed full of valuable information that will help you be more successful, because you will be able to better understand your thought processes and the decisions you need to make.

Sack Your Boss by **Christian Rodwell**

This book will help you to get to know yourself better, identifying your motives for wanting to leave your job and answering the question "What would I love to do each day if money were no object?" Chris has been through all of these challenges himself, and has worked with over 1,000 other 'escapees' who are on the same journey.

1.5 Choosing the Right Teacher/s

'Doing your due diligence' became a mantra for our year, and we started early on when choosing the right teacher. My core values include honesty, helping others, adventure, commitment and energy. So when I went along to some of the free events and spoke to training companies, I would really use my gut instinct and understand whether their values truly resonated with mine. One organisation proffered the advice that we could buy a house with a credit card – I walked out there and then! But for others that might just be the catalyst to their journey; we are all very different people and can make our own choices in life.

In our decision, both John and I felt that the honest, ethical and supported approach of the one we chose, alongside it matching our learning styles and offering accountability support too, made the decision easy. It wasn't the cheapest, but we knew that if we were seriously going to make this work, the choice of teacher was critical, not the price.

Take your time to decide and never be rushed into buying a course. I attended a few events where you were heavily 'sold to' in the room – sometimes being encouraged to run to the back of the room for the one amazing offer today only! It's so easy to be swept up in the frenzy of this, but I must say you will always have a cooling-off period by law, so if this happens, there is a way out.

Finally, my advice is that if the person or organisation is truly ethical and believes in their product, then they should offer a get-out clause after a certain period of time. The company we used had a money-back guarantee on the introductory three-day course. If by halfway through the course you didn't feel it was value for money, then you could leave the materials behind and get your money back. On my online programme, I also offer a refund if after the first 30 days you realise it's not for you.

So now you've got a compelling 'reason why' that you're excited about, you've set some initial goals and you've researched who might help you learn. How about I share with you now the first ever buy-to-let property we did and how the numbers worked.

CASE STUDY 1: Buy to let

UPPER BROOK STREET – Two-bed ex-council maisonette

This was our first rental property, bought as a single-let maisonette above a shop in the middle of Winchester. We had no education in property investing at this stage and were lucky that in fact the numbers stacked pretty well. However, with hindsight, it could have been risky because with a 75% interest-only mortgage and looking at the cash flow numbers, just a couple of months empty and we'd be in the negative.

So, the real risk in a single-let property with a mortgage is that if you can't rent it for any reason then the council tax and utilities (as well as the mortgage) become your responsibility, and that is a real problem for cash flow.

Objective: Get a higher return on our savings with potential capital growth in the long term. We hoped to get 5% minimum return on the funds we put in.

Strategy: Single-let flat right in the city centre with two double bedrooms.

How did we find the property? High street estate agent.

Position of the vendor: This property was empty, had been on the market for a while, and the owner had just decided to take it off. We stepped in just in time.

Funding: The estate agent sorted out the mortgage, insurance and management. Deposit was from equity.

Workload: Professional clean, new blinds on the windows and a full painting and redecoration.

Issues: Leasehold – but an ex-council maisonette above shops and it had a very long lease.

No parking, but so far that's not stopped demand given its city centre location.

Numbers:

Asking price: £225,000 (Sept 2013)
Offered: £215,000

Mortgage	£159,000
Deposit	£53,000

Costs:

Stamp duty	£2,120
Conveyancing	£1,018
Mortgage fee	£180
Legal fees & admin	£962
Total purchase costs	**£4,280**

Mortgage fees:

Broker's fee	£550

Valuation	£167
Admin	£75
Arrangement fee	£1,495
(added on to the mortgage)	
CHAPS fee	£30
(deducted from mortgage advance)	
	£2,317
Refurbishment	**£2,000**
Capital outlay	**£60,072**
Monthly rental gross:	**£1,050**

Monthly operating costs:

Mortgage	£506
Insurance	£12
Agent	**£95**
Total monthly average costs	**£614**

Net profit per month   **£436**
(no voids – times between tenancies)

Return on capital invested (ROI):
(£436*12)/(£60,072) = 8.7%

Plus points:

- The agent was very helpful as we were new to investing.

- Only a light refurbishment was needed to be able to rent it out.

- Location was mid-city – perfect for rental demand.

Lessons learned:

- A single buy-to-let isn't hard to do and the costs per month are low as the tenant pays for council tax, utilities and contents.

- Costs of the mortgage were higher than we thought.

- Check out the lease if buying a flat; there could be restrictions and clauses that cause problems.

Current situation: This property continues to rent very well given its location and having two bedrooms. At some point we will need to upgrade the bathroom and kitchen to keep it modern and keep the rental price high. Capital growth looks likely too.

This example shows that you can take advice from others and learn on the go, but the very next thing we did was to start worrying about what responsibilities we were taking on as landlords. Whilst others can advise you, we felt we needed to really understand the subject and to manage the potential risks. After all, there will be someone living in a property we own, signing a tenancy agreement, etc. What happens if something goes wrong?

This was the point at which I said "Let's buy a book." A couple of Amazon best sellers later and we found the book *Property Magic* by Simon Zutshi. Whilst we thought we would just need to read about landlords' responsibilities, the book told us that there are ways to create much higher returns than our mere 8% (and lower with voids). We started researching. Then a whole new world of property education opened up – lots of amazing statements were being made and they all sounded too good to be true! But if there is some way to continue getting rental income from several properties, maybe that 'freedom' we were seeking could be possible.

Finding an education that suits your learning style, pocket and time is the first step to success. There are many providers out there, but our choice after the research was Simon Zutshi's Property Mastermind Programme. Much of what I'll be sharing has come from the teachings from this ten-month programme, and I will attribute this to Simon who remains a good friend and supporter.

Try to find someone who you can relate to in your learning. The learning style for me needed to be face to face, visual, active and with groups of people. I also need accountability, coaching and mentoring types of support; to make sure that I took the action needed, I had someone I could talk to regularly and work through issues with as I went along.

The economics of the UK property market makes it an attractive place to invest. There are ways to borrow money from both banks and individuals, and there are ways to provide a return to those lenders. Just make sure you have the best education to understand and minimise the risks that do exist.

CHAPTER 2:

ERECTING THE SUPPORTING WALLS

STEP 2.
Put Your Plan Into Action

"A dream written down with a date becomes a goal. A goal broken down into steps becomes a plan. A plan backed by action makes your dreams come true."

Greg S. Reid

It's all very well having the dreams and goals, but in a way that's the easy bit. The hard bit is working out how to make them a reality. In this section, I'm going to share with you what worked for me, and some of the things I found hard and struggled with but discovered ways to manage. It really is so easy to give up and find excuses to not progress, especially if you're working and have family commitments. Practical ideas for both time management and money elements are critical as they tend to be the main reasons why people give up. There are also the inherent lessons taught by generations that debt is a bad thing. I'll beg to differ from this opinion, as it depends what the borrowing is for.

2.1 Accountability and Support

I knew at the beginning of our education in property that to be able to really make progress I had to have someone holding my hand – someone nudging me and holding me to account. My style of learning is to see and do – a visual style. Unless I actually took physical action to do the tasks I was learning about, then I would quickly forget and have to revise what I'd learned. Others I know would prefer to learn as much as they can to get all the information before taking action, or are self-driven and super motivated. We are all different. But if John and I were to achieve the goals we set, grow in confidence and progress, we would have to achieve some results early on.

In order to take those actions though, I needed to have written them down and prioritised them. At each monthly learning session, I would write down a specific action – no matter how small – and then at the end of the day take time to prioritise those actions. But then how did I make sure they got done? With my job at the time taking me to the Isle of Wight four days a week – a round trip of three hours – I knew that I would be time poor. So it was important to use the time around my job and get those actions done.

The answer for me was regular one-to-one coaching, and this would happen every two weeks over the phone. My coach agreed with me early on what coaching style I preferred. That could mean being tough, holding me to account and being really hard on me. Or it could mean being supportive, empathetic and encouraging, or something in between. For this to really work for me, I needed to know that I was being held to account too. Did I do the tasks I had set for myself? Had I made progress? That way, I would make sure that I prepared and also had some questions to ask so that I could use my coach's experience too.

When you look for coaching, make sure you find someone you relate to, who is successful in their own right in the specific property strategy you are focusing on. Try them out and agree that you will both review things after a couple of sessions. Don't forget this is your journey, your money and your progress. Make sure it's working for you.

2.2 Time Management

Time is the most common excuse I hear and it was one I struggled with myself. How on earth could I find the time in my busy life to be learning and looking for properties? But when I worked through what I spent my time doing, and really challenged myself, then it was possible to find solutions. Let me give you some examples:

Commuting – time in the car or on the train – an hour or two each day

TV – an hour or two each day

Reading the Sunday paper – an hour or two each week

Cleaning – a couple of hours each weekend

Gardening – an hour or three on weekends – of course seasonal

Ironing – an hour or two rarely – work shirts and blouses

Washing/drying – an hour or two each week

Sleeping – important – I like my seven hours – but I could get up earlier perhaps

Pilates/yoga/circuits – two or three hours a week

Walking neighbour's dog – one hour a week

Which of these can you sacrifice? How might you get someone else to do the cleaning/ironing for you (for a fee of course)? I even recruited my children at times to help with the daily chores – quite right too!

In my situation, I had my commuting time. I'd listen to podcasts in the car, replay the learning modules and listen to motivational speakers. I stopped the TV watching, realising that I could capture around eight hours a week! In my lunch hours I'd nip out to talk to estate agents or view a property in the area. My coaching calls I'd do early in the morning, generally before work. The one thing I would never give up though is my fitness and yoga sessions, which kept me sane, as did walking in the countryside on a nice day or going out with the family for a fun day.

In my book list in 1.4 above you will see a number of books on how to manage time – you can see what my big issue was! Find one that resonates with you that you can really put into practice. It takes a lot of discipline and focus, which is where your 'reason why' comes to the fore to keep you motivated.

2.3 Funding

Money – oh my goodness! This is what stops most people in their tracks. So here I want to be very clear that there are plenty of ways of finding funding. Much of the issue early on is understanding the risks and your own risk profile – that is, what level of risk you are comfortable with.

Mortgages

Remember the lessons of the previous generation, and my parents were no exception, that to pay off your mortgage as soon as possible was a key aim? I'm going to challenge this because for me it's all about what is a true asset. Of course paying off the mortgage on your home leaves you with less outgoings in repayments, but your own home is not a cash-flowing asset that creates income. It's much more of a liability because of the upkeep and costs that come with it. Now, also depending on the economy, the interest rates and costs of borrowing vary, but mortgage rates are generally the cheapest form of large-scale borrowing there is in the UK, as I outlined in 1.1 above.

Buy-to-let mortgages are generally easy to obtain on investment properties as long as the numbers stack up. Banks are comfortable with the opportunity property provides for rental profit and capital growth, and will lend for well beyond 25 years and with no issue with the borrower's age either. It's more a business transaction. For certain strategies, you'll need advice from a mortgage broker. Lenders need to know what your planned strategy is and a broker will have specialist knowledge of the right product to suit you.

There is a way to manage the interest rate risk too by fixing the rate for a number of years. Usually there are two, five- and ten-year fixed rates. Fixing it gives you security to know that the rate will not change. If interest rates rise or fall, your rate will remain the same.

Private Investors – loans and joint ventures

Many people say to me that they have money but very quickly run out after the first one or two investments. Deposits of 25% and capital needed for refurbishment eat into funds fast. So how were we able to press on with building our portfolio? Well, it's been all about working with other people's money and finding a win-win situation

– helping someone get a great return for their money that might be sitting in low-yielding savings accounts, whilst then enabling a property purchase to take place using my skills and knowledge. Yes, I'd be paying them a return for their money, reducing my profitability, but that's much better than no profit at all if I didn't even purchase the property!

Working with other people's money is a big responsibility and trust needs to be built up over time, making sure to understand what that individual wants and needs from their money. It's never a case of asking someone directly for funds. The key is to tell as many people as you can about what you are doing and then to show them some examples of how the returns on investment can be made. Then it's about understanding their risk profile, how long they'd be happy to tie up their money for and other needs if it reaches that point in discussion.

Some of my best investors have been people I've known before in my career – friends and family who know me well or people who have been introduced to me by others. I've also met people at property meetings and other business networking events. Building trust is a two-way street. Can they get on with me and know my level of experience, my values and my track record, whilst I'm looking for the same from them? Our skills will be different, but can we work together in a business relationship to benefit each other? Do they have £5,000 in a bank they might lend for just a few months, or do they have £50,000 sitting in a business they're happy to tie up for a few years or more? Do they want a fixed return or would they be happy to share the profit in a deal in a joint venture (JV)? What security are they comfortable with? The percentage rate of interest is of course negotiable. The fact that savings rates in the banks have been so low in the UK makes it a more compelling opportunity for those with cash in the bank. There is a lot of frustration for savers to try to find better returns.

Let me share some examples from both extremes. I used LinkedIn to reconnect with people I'd worked with in the past to let them know what I was doing. If any of them expressed an interest, I'd share a few nuggets with them as to how the rental market can work.

Jack had worked with me in the bank and said he was fed up with the low savings rates and share values. I called him and we chatted through a few things, then met up for coffee. I had created a presentation folder with some examples of the deals I'd done, including pictures and numbers. This meant if it was the right time in the conversation I could open it up and show him how the returns could be created and how an investor could achieve a high return on investment. As we'd worked together for quite a few years, the trust was there. He was keen to try out a small investment for cash flow purposes for six months at an interest rate much higher than in a bank savings account. Following on from this he invested more and for longer, enabling me to use these funds for future projects.

The boiler in our home needed to be serviced and so I had to take time off work to be around to let the engineer in. Making him tea, I mentioned that I was learning about property investing and his ears pricked up. We ended up having a long chat about the market and his interest in the subject. He'd been to some property network meetings in the past. We subsequently met up quite a few times as he followed our progress, coming to see our finished houses. One day, I was showing potential investors around a property and he came too. Then he asked if he might invest with us. I didn't know he might be considering that, so we moved on to the next level of investing that gave him what he was looking for. Now he's earning many multiples of what he was getting in the bank!

A very important part of the responsibility of borrowing from others is the paperwork and being as professional as possible. Yes, I had been a banker and I understood the importance of loan agreements and security, but just a simple summary of the plan (known in legal terms as a 'heads of terms') and then a document you both contribute to and sign is critical – even if it's a family member. Time after time I hear stories of people falling out over something so simple that it could have been dealt with early on. It's not worth it. Communicate clearly and effectively and in writing, then there is no argument later. Document the term of the loan, the notice needed to return funds and 'What happens if …' scenarios. Even though you think it will never happen, it can and does – believe me.

Here are the key areas you would usually include in a heads of terms:

Names of the lender and borrower

Loan sum: Generally we borrow between £10,000 and £100,000

Purpose: Cash flow, purchase, development, refurbishment

Repayment plan: The project should have options – usually at least two, e.g. refinance or sell

Term: 6-18 months depending on the project – always overestimate

Interest rate: 4%-12%pa – depending on the investor's need, the project risk and value-add the project is delivering

Interest payment: Usually interest is paid at the end of the project with the capital repayment, although some longer-term loans we've paid quarterly

Security: Depends on the project and risk. Can be a personal guarantee, deed of trust, second charge on a property or nothing at all

Other things you think are important to include: e.g. options to extend the term if late payment, notice period of early redemption, etc.

Joint ventures are very different from loans. Here you agree to work together in a specific deal, and share the responsibilities and the upside profit or the downside loss. It's a business relationship where all parties contribute something of value. In the simple scenario it could be funds for the purchase and refurbishment only, and we the property expert find and manage the property project. We did several of these in our first two years because we had run out of our own money. For the right investor with the right experience and risk appetite this works well.

Pension Funds

This is a pretty specialist area, but I'd been talking to a potential investor who said he'd like to use his Self-Invested Personal Pension (SIPP) to invest in a project. This opened our eyes up to the world of entrepreneur's pensions where the owner is able to take responsibility for investing their funds – within strict HMRC rules. The other type of pension that is also able to lend is the Small Self-Administered Scheme (SSAS).

These loans are still private loans from an individual; it's just where they source the money from that's different. Loans with pension funds must have good security offered, usually a first charge or a personal guarantee. We'd built our portfolio to a size where, along with our home, we had a good diversified asset base with equity, so we were able to borrow through this source to fund some of our deals. You'll see these mentioned in the case studies throughout this book.

Nurturing the investor relationship is really important as circumstances change for both you and them. We've had longer term joint venture partners happy to park their money in a multi-let property, and then need the funds back after a couple of years. Also we've had a loan investor that pulled out just before exchange on a property. Things happen and contingency needs to be in place.

Bridging Loans

A bridging loan is a short-term loan against a property, usually up to 18 months. This allows a property that needs specific work done to add value, or perhaps to convert to a different type of dwelling, to be refinanced or sold. For example, a house that isn't mortgageable because it has a structural issue or needs a big refurbishment can be financed and then remortgaged on to the longer-term product such as a buy-to-let mortgage. I mention the bridging loan because it was often something we had as a back-up on deals we were doing, in case private finance wasn't raised in time.

Funding must take into account all the costs of refurbishing a property, including the use of experts and specialists to investigate issues such as damp and structural problems.

2.4 Tax

There's nothing exciting about tax, although some people might like the fact that it's usually paid on the profit created, so that's a good thing to have profit isn't it? Basically if you buy, own, sell or inherit property in the UK, there are a number of tax facts you need to be aware of.

I'll cover just the basics here and mention some relevant tax laws later that are worth noting. Things do change with the government budgets and regulations, so always check the most up to date information. To overcome the complexity, it's essential in my view to take advice from a specialist property accountant. Everyone's personal tax position is different and if you're currently a high or low rate tax payer in a corporate job, this will of course have an impact on your property business.

Stamp Duty

Stamp duty land tax, also known as SDLT or just stamp duty, was originally introduced in 2003 and revised in 2014 and 2015. It is payable on the purchase of British land and property. For self-builders, stamp duty is payable on land but not on build costs. SDLT applies to the majority of sales and transfers of land or property.

Buy-to-let/second home higher stamp duty rates and thresholds

From April 2016, anyone buying a second property in the UK, including a buy-to-let property, would pay an additional 3% on top of the relevant standard rate band.

The rates and thresholds are:

- 0% on properties under £40,000

- 3% between £0 and £125,000 (unless the property is below £40,000)

- 5% between £125,000 and £250,000

- 8% between £250,000 and £925,000

- 13% between £925,000 £1,500,000

- 15% on anything over £1,500,000

These new figures came in after our first year of investing, so the case study figures in this book will vary. The rates may well change in future government budgets.

Income Tax on UK Property

Income from British property is taxable as income in the UK and there is an income tax-free personal allowance for individuals.

However, your personal tax-free allowance goes down by £1 for every £2 that your adjusted net income is above £100,000, meaning your personal allowance is zero if your income is £122,000 or above.

Income tax for landlords

Up until the 2016/17 tax year, landlords could deduct mortgage interest and other allowable costs from their rental income, before calculating their tax liability.

From 6 April 2020, tax relief for finance costs will be restricted to the basic rate of income tax, currently 20%. Relief will be given as a reduction in tax liability instead of a reduction to taxable rental income. The changes started to be phased in from April 2017.

Deductions

As a landlord you can deduct 'allowable' expenses before your tax bill is calculated.

These include:

- Mortgage interest costs (until the new rules stated above are applied)

- Maintenance costs

- Lettings agent fees

- Insurance premiums

- Council tax where applicable

- Utility bills where applicable

Your income tax rate will depend on your net income, i.e. after costs.

The type of specialist advice gained through a property accountant will help with the difference between capital costs and revenue costs.

Capital costs include items such as boilers, radiators, kitchen suites, bathroom suites and electrical systems. Revenue costs include things like painting and decorating, damp treatment, mending broken windows, doors, furniture, replacing roof slates and guttering. These can be offset against your profit and therefore reduces your tax liability. To get a more detailed list there is plenty of guidance on the HMRC website.

You can reduce tax through:

- Buying significantly below the market value

- Refurbishing through repairs and replacement of existing assets

- Refinancing the property to take funds out and buy another property

2.5 Leasing Contents

When refurbishing a property there are a lot of expenses that when you add them up can be pretty high if you're wanting a new and modern look. To support cash flow there are ways of renting the furnishings and white goods over a period of time, the costs of which can also be offset against profit to reduce tax. We chose to lease the white goods and TVs in our HMOs, because it spread the cost as well as provided an insurance for breakdown and replacement. We've looked at furnishing our guest houses through leasing too and assessed the pros and cons of an upfront cost or borrowing with the associated tax benefits. It's often worth considering, especially if you require new items rather than second hand.

2.6 Different Property Investing Strategies

If you've done any research into the subject, you are likely to feel overwhelmed by the choices out there. The key here is to take your goals, work out which strategy will work best for those goals and your risk profile, and focus on just the one strategy that feels right for you. It's sensible to start with simple buy-to-lets to gain your confidence and expertise. It's the simplest and the most hands-off strategy out there.

As we mastered the basics and grew our knowledge and confidence, new opportunities and strategies reared their heads. Our aims in finding properties were to seek out motivated sellers and create opportunities for a win-win situation where we could help with problems and also benefit from the deal. We also needed to understand how to fund the deals and to consider investors and even pension fund investments. Here are a few strategies that we used early on in our investing.

Multi-let Strategy or Houses of Multiple Occupation

Houses that can be shared by people who are not related to each other, for example student houses, are generally known as houses of multiple occupation (HMOs). Many people will have had experience of these types of arrangements, either themselves as students or their own children. This strategy comes with a lot of rules and regulations, particularly with regard to many city centres that have restricted their growth in certain areas by putting in planning rules. There are often licensing processes so councils can police standards too.

We started with this strategy as it can be the highest cash-flowing opportunity. You will have five or six people each paying rent for a room with shared facilities. That will usually be much more than if it was let as a single let. There is also a growing demand for young professionals who are starting work and want to live with friends but in a much nicer property than when they were students. They can afford to live closer to work if they share a house too. Each tenant has their own tenancy agreement. There are pros and cons of this strategy.

- If one person leaves, there are still others to provide an income to cover your bills.

- You can choose whether to include bills for the tenants or not. This depends on the tenant type and your preference for making things as easy as possible.

- Students generally have guarantors for their rent so there is unlikely to be a loss of rent on default.

- If you aim at providing high-end properties for say young professionals, with ensuites, Sky TV package etc. the returns can be very high.

Cons:

- There is much more work and cost upfront to create the facilities. For example, the property needs to be fully furnished with fire doors, fire alarm system, bathrooms/ensuites, white goods, TVs and all the kitchen equipment. A good fast broadband is a necessity for multiple users too.

- Planning regulations and licensing requirements must be understood.

- There will be more wear and tear on furnishings than a single let.

- A specialist type of mortgage product is needed.

Freehold to Leasehold

This is a strategy that enables a large freehold property to be split up into smaller properties that each have their own lease. Obviously that would involve planning permission, and a pretty big refurbishment/conversion involving each dwelling being self-contained, with its own utility supplies, etc. You can often see these types of property conversions in a terraced house where the upstairs is split from the downstairs.

It's a really useful strategy to have when viewing unusually large properties, or to have as a Plan B in case of need.

Pros:

- Creating a separate dwelling adds significant value to a property – two one-bed flats tend to be worth more than a two-bed house.

- This can give an efficient use of large floor spaces to create additional living areas.

- The freehold element of the property has a value too and can be retained or sold.

Cons:

- There will be legal costs of splitting the title.

- The refurbishment costs can be high and will require splitting the utilities to have their own meters.

- The freeholder continues to take responsibility for much of the structure of the property – there will be specific rules written into the lease in this regard.

Holiday Letting (sometimes known as Serviced Accommodation)

This strategy provides a property as a short-term let, from a single night to a few weeks. Depending on the location, it could be for short-term breaks, contractors working in a city, or holidaymakers.

The rent is paid on a per-night basis, and tends to be much higher than if it were a single let. Consider when you've looked at Booking.com or Airbnb to find an overnight stay; these platforms and others give a good idea of what this strategy entails. Clearly it's much more effort because it will be fully furnished, full linen supplied, the all-important wi-fi and all the mod cons needed.

If you've yearned after a holiday place yourself – be it home or abroad – then maybe it's worth considering this strategy. You can use it yourself and even plan to retire there in the future.

Pros:

- Charging per night and in the right area the rental income will be much higher than a single let.

- Rent can be varied for seasonal demand.

- Even with voids this can provide more profit than a single let.

- Less wear and tear on the property than a single let.

- Tax efficient as the mortgage interest is allowable against profit (see the tax changes mentioned above).

Cons:

- There is much more effort in the management of pricing and bookings.

- Cost and effort in change-overs, cleaning, laundry, etc. You may need to use someone locally to manage it for you.

- Capital cost of being fully furnished, and installing fire alarm systems, insurance etc.

- All bills are paid by the owner.

- A specialist type of mortgage is needed.

Here's a case study of the first deal we did after we had started our property education.

CASE STUDY 2:
Buying our first multi-let property

ALFRED STREET – Five-bed terraced house run as an HMO

Objective: To achieve a high monthly cash flow – return on capital invested (ROI) greater than 15%.

Strategy: HMO for workers in Southampton city centre – a monthly rate per room can achieve a much higher rental per month and give flexibility in terms of risk of voids.

The definition of an HMO for licensing purposes is any property occupied by five or more people, forming two or more separate households. A household is generally 'a family'; for example, a couple is one household.

Mandatory licensing applies to houses with five or more people sharing, and is in place to make sure standards, quality and the safety of shared housing is maintained. This includes things like size of bedrooms, communal space, number of bathrooms, and gas and fire safety. Each council is slightly different, so it's always worth checking on the website of the council where the property is located for their interpretation.

Recent planning legislation is trying to manage the number of HMO type houses in specific city centre areas due to the community change that can result. For example, streets near to universities have been changed from quiet family areas to busy term-time streets with multiple cars and more noise. To do this, some geographic areas in cities have been set aside as 'Article 4' areas, where there is planning permission required to convert a house into an HMO.

This isn't a strategy for novices. A good education is essential to avoid risks of not meeting legislative requirements or not calculating the additional costs that wouldn't be incurred if it were a single let (council tax, insurance, utilities and broadband).

How did we find the property? Through an estate agent that I'd been getting to know. I had already viewed several properties with him, pointing out what wasn't quite right with them. Building rapport, and teaching him what I was looking for, led to him calling me directly about this one early in its listing on the Rightmove portal. He told me there was going to be an open day on the following Saturday. Now that's a no-no in my book – too much competition and that could push up the price. So I told him that I could view it the next day (with John too) and that we'd love to meet the owner as he was currently running it as an HMO.

Position of the vendor: Current owners were looking to retire and use the money to travel.

Funding: We remortgaged our home to release equity to use as deposits on the first few properties. 25% deposit, with an HMO specialised 25-year interest-only mortgage.

Workload: Very little work was needed as it already conformed to the licensing requirements – fire doors, hand basins in rooms, bathroom and fire alarm. All we needed to do was remove old furniture, have the carpets cleaned, install new window blinds and buy new beds.

Issues: There was no communal area and the kitchen wasn't very big either. It suited workers in the area of the city. One long-term tenant was still in situ – we agreed to continue his tenure if he signed a new assured shorthold tenancy agreement with us. Our specialist letting agent dealt with the advertising of rooms, tenancy agreements and any light refurb such as redecoration, furniture, new mattresses, etc. He advised us with his investor experience too.

Numbers:

Asking price: £170,000 (Feb 2014)
Offered: £170,000
(with the condition he took it off the market)

Stamp duty	£3,400

(2% – before revised additional rates
mentioned in tax above)

Legal costs	£427
Deposit funds	£42,500
Refurb one-off	£1,770
Total capital in	**£44,697**

Monthly rental gross:	**£1,778**

Monthly operating costs:

Mortgage	£465
Council tax	£102
Utilities	£222

(Water £62 +Gas/Elec £160)

Broadband	£25
Insurance	£51
Agent	£215

(incl cleaning £15pw & maintenance)

Total monthly costs	**£1,080**

Annual costs:

Gas safety	£60
Fire safety	£80
Garden	£100
TV licence	£145

(for communal area)

HMO licence	£245
(£490 every 2 years)	
Total av pm	**£52**
Total monthly av costs	**£1,132**
Net profit per month	**£646**
(no voids)	

Return on capital invested (ROI):
(£646 *12)/(£44,697) = 17.3%

Plus points:

- An existing HMO in Southampton, run by a landlord who had a licence and seemed to be operating it professionally. Made it easy as a first purchase as we didn't have to convert it.

- Planning permission as an HMO had been granted – C4 category (as it's in an Article 4 area).

- We'd done our homework on the locations we'd been researching, looked at the numbers of purchase and rental income, and built up a rapport with the agent.

- Location was good, and not too far from a hospital and local shops. On-street parking.

- We knew exactly what return on investment the property would give us at the asking price, given the rental agreements already in place. This exceeded our goal of 15% ROI.

The next step was being able to secure it against the competition, which we did by avoiding the open day, meeting the owner and offering ahead of the event.

Lessons learned:

- It's great to learn from something already set up and working. It's good to work through the actual numbers in reality rather than estimates.

- There were more costs than we thought at the beginning as we'd forgotten some of the annual costs and licensing costs, which have been rising every year.

- Although there were hand basins in the rooms, we felt that one bathroom wasn't really enough.

- If we had a possibility of adding value – extending or going into the roof to make an additional sixth room and another bathroom – the monthly income could be improved. Our following purchases were six-bed properties for this reason.

Current situation: After this purchase, we focused on more upmarket larger properties with more space, as we felt this property wasn't of the standard we were aiming for. There was no possibility of extending the property to create the space needed. We sold it as an existing HMO in September 2017 for £226,000 (an uplift of £56,000 in three and a half years).

What a difference this example is compared to the first deal we did before our learning started. At the time, we felt confident: we used the lessons learned from our training, and with the coaching as support too, we were very well prepared to make an offer. We came across as confident to the estate agent and to the vendor, all of which came together to seal our first over-10% return on investment.

It sounds so easy when you see it written down like this, but let's not forget that there were many viewings before we found this one, many spreadsheets tested out and many sleepless nights worrying about this next step. It's those fears I'm going to come on to now, as overcoming them is the difference between taking action or not.

CHAPTER 3:

RAISING THE ROOF

STEP 3.
What Happens If...?

"I learned that courage was not the absence of fear, but the triumph over it. The brave man is not he who does not feel afraid, but he who conquers that fear."

Nelson Mandela

A big part of property investing learning is dealing with money, debt and risk. Luckily, both John and I had a bit of experience under our belts, and also as a career banker I'd grown up with much of this basic understanding. That didn't make me risk happy necessarily, but I certainly understood that borrowing low and creating an income that exceeded the repayments was a sensible thing.

There were lots of hopes and fears when we started out and they were different between John and me. It was only through understanding and learning, and having experts with experience to support us, that we gained the confidence to overcome them. Then once you've started out, you've extended your comfort zone to move on to the next zone!

This section will help you see that it's normal to feel scared, and it's normal to have things go wrong, but it's only by doing it that you really learn.

3.1 Understanding Your Fears

Now it's not just money and debt that create fear. It's the little voice in your head that says "I can't do it – it's too hard" or that says "You'll never be able to do…" whatever that might be. How do you overcome that? The acronym I use is that fear can stand for:

False

Expectations

Appearing

Real

So until you can understand why it might be a false expectation in your eyes and really learn the reality through an education, it's hard to change. It's also a mindset thing. If you are surrounded by people who are negative and don't necessarily have the knowledge, then you will just accept it as fact.

Here's a list of the most pressing concerns I had and I still hear frequently from my clients who are starting out.

Problem:

- Estate agents – they'll see me as not being serious. They know more than me. What if I say the wrong thing? What if…?

Solution:

- Get to know a high street agent and ask them for help and advice. They've usually been in the game a while, know the area well and want your business too.

- For me, it was to listen to my coach and my course suggestions of how to approach an agent, what to say and memorise those first few questions. I needed to remember to praise the agent and tell them that I really needed to tap into their amazing knowledge of the area. Then it was nurturing the relationship into the future by popping in with gifts of doughnuts! This usually worked a treat!

- When we actually bought a property through them, I'd be round on completion day to pick up the keys and take them a box of wine and cakes to share. I was certainly going to be remembered by the whole team!

Problem:

- Bank borrowing – my own home is at risk if I default or can't afford to pay the loan.

- Is remortgaging our own home to have the starting capital a risk?

Solution:

- Well of course it is – but it's only when you hear it that you can feel really worried. I always revert to the numbers and the contingency, ask my coach/mentor to be a sounding board and then ask myself "What's the worst that can happen? Can I sell the property without needing to revert to my security?"

- Remember that a property is an asset: it has a value and can create an income. As long as you follow some basic rules and buy in an area of high rental demand, then there are always options.

Problem:

- Rental tenants – what if the tenants trash the house or room and steal all the furniture?

Solution:

- It can happen, but it's rare. You tend to hear about the worst case stories from others, but if you have a good agent and good tenancy agreements, with regular visits planned ahead, then you can be reassured. Don't forget that tenants in single lets tend to look after somewhere they love and want to stay in. If you don't provide clean and tidy houses the psychology can be that the tenant doesn't look after it so well.

- Use a really good agent who makes sure checks have been carried out, deposits taken and contracts signed. Regular communication and discussions are important.

- It's happened to us but in an HMO situation. There is sometimes one rogue who falls behind with the rent and then struggles. They don't always want to listen to reason and may take offence. Factor these costs into your calculations and assume it will happen on occasion.

Problem:

- Letting agents – what if my agent runs off with all our money and defrauds me?

Solution:

- There are the big high street agents who most people tend to use. Then there are private agents who are experts too. They're harder to find but you can meet them at networking events or through other landlords in the area.

Check out their qualifications and professional affiliations, such as the Association of Residential Letting Agents (ARLA) or the Guild of Lettings and Management. Make sure they are qualified and really know the latest changes in tenant laws.

- Get to know the agent ahead of choosing to work with them. Talk to people who use them, arrange to meet them for coffee outside of their office environment.

- In my experience, see whether their values align with yours, how they look after their own properties if they are agents who are also property investors themselves.

Problem:

- Investors – what if I can't pay them back?

Solution:

- It's a big responsibility and of course you will worry about making sure you look after their funds. This can be managed through very clear agreements in writing, clarity of what might happen in certain scenarios, and contingency discussions. It's all about the numbers and making sure the whole deal will work.

- Keep up regular communication, good and not so good. If there's been a delay in the refurb, or the project hasn't gone to plan, then you must keep investors informed.

- One of our development projects was delayed by over a year when we were refused planning permission. All our investors continued with us as we explained and reassured them of our position and plans.

Problem:

- Money – leaving my corporate job behind and the fixed monthly salary that arrives in my bank without me having to think too much about it. Scary.

Solution:

- Well that's what being an entrepreneur is all about. If you plan and build the business slowly while still working for someone else, you can start to let go as the income builds. That way, you aren't putting pressure on yourself from Day 1. I reduced the hours I worked and was honest with my employers about my plans. They were very supportive and I didn't feel too guilty when I needed time off for my own business.

- Don't forget you can always get another job. Once you've tasted the freedom of being your own boss and making your own choices for your future, you will not look back.

- Big plus point is that I became a lower rate taxpayer, improving my net profit position.

Problem:

- How do I start networking to learn more and meet other investors when I have no experience yet?

Solution:

- Just start anyway. Find out where there are property network meetings nearby – usually you can just Google 'property network meetings in …' and there will be some that pop up.

- Attend the meetings local to you and your chosen investing area. You'll be surprised to hear that there are a lot of first-time people in the room, all looking nervous. Go with an open mind and see how it feels.

- My experience was a positive one, but it took a few meetings to start to feel more comfortable. Once you realise that you are with people who are positive and knowledgeable and who can inspire and motivate you, you'll want to do more.

- Try not to feel inferior. Go prepared with some business cards and don't talk to one person for too long – take their details and follow up with them later. Meeting and chatting to people after the event over coffee or on the phone is a better use of time.

Problem:

- Tax – I've heard that changes in the tax treatment of buy-to-let property have made investing unprofitable.

Solution:

- Section 24 of the Finance Act 2015 introduced a significant change for finance costs. What it means is that you will no longer be able to claim mortgage interest, or any other property finance, as tax deductible. The changes were phased in gradually over four years, starting from 5th April 2017. By 2020, 100% of finance costs will be restricted to 20% tax relief only.

- If you are a higher rate tax payer or are close to being one, this could have a big impact. My advice is to speak with a specialist property tax accountant who can look at your specific situation.

- There are ways to mitigate some of the impacts, including choosing the best strategy where this doesn't apply, or buying in a limited company.

A lot of fears can be started through what we read in the press and social media. It was one thing we learned early on and that was to stop reading newspapers as they are so negative. News stories abound with property rental nightmares; they even make TV programmes about it. You can flip this and start spending time with successful property investors – people who are investing now and have experience – and join the positive groups on social media. But take care, as sometimes these can also be negative or misleading.

This is where good coaching and mentoring can also help. Not only is it for accountability as mentioned before, but it is also for crisis and 'FEAR' moments. My top tips for overcoming these include listening to the topic in a learning module or on audio. Before I visited an estate agent the first few times I'd listen to the audio of the module reminding me about the key questions to ask and to feel confident just before going in. Much of the fear can be overcome by using common sense and understanding how in the learning process. It shouldn't be a reason for not starting.

3.2 The 'First Time' Syndrome

Looking back, it was the 'first time' situation that was the hardest, and I hear it often with my clients too.

The first time talking to an estate agent – they'll see right through me – they know more than me… What if they ask me something I don't know?

The first buy-to-let mortgage – you are seen as a novice, the interest rate is higher as a consequence and the fees seem to reflect that too! As soon as you do the next one, you are deemed 'experienced'! Crazy but true.

The first time you fill a house with tenants… Will they pay on time? Will they trash the place? Will they grow cannabis in the loft?

The first refurbishment project – you don't know what you don't know. Consequently, we overran and overspent. But the learning was amazing. To overcome this, we worked with an experienced team and built up the 'power team' we could trust to help us.

The first holiday let – will anyone ever want to holiday here?

The first time borrowing from a private investor – a scary moment, realising you are responsible for more than just your own assets.

The first time securing a bridging loan – the solicitor sits you down and says all your assets are at risk if you default. You have to sign to say you've been told. You feel like a naughty toddler caught in the act.

All of these can be overcome by having a good education in investing, and a coach or mentor to hold your hand and guide you, reassuring you along the way. Otherwise there will be paralysis and no action taken to progress.

3.3 Stretching Your Comfort Zone

To progress in life, there will always be times when you will be going beyond your 'comfort zone' as it's often referred to. It could be the smallest thing – getting through the test at school, climbing your first tree, taking the stabilisers off the bike, or the biggest thing – parachuting, climbing Everest, or building a business. It's about moving beyond what is 'normal' for you, facing a challenge, and in some cases overcoming the fear.

We've all experienced it in our lives. The key thing when you look back is that it never seems quite so bad after the event, and it can of course be a huge boost to confidence too.

But it isn't a matter of just closing your eyes and going for it! That's pretty mad. It's much more about getting your mindset ready, doing the preparation and making sure you don't leap too far in one go. I like the model that describes the different circles around your current 'comfort circle' as the Fear Zone, Learning Zone and Growth Zone. Whatever works for you, there are plenty of articles written about this online.

My advice from my property journey is to break down the issue into smaller pieces – baby-size steps if you like. Getting the best education you can about the particular area is a great starting point. This will help you understand the true risks and give you confidence. A question my parents often asked me when I was a child was "What's the worst thing that could happen?" I often revert to this question for myself and in my coaching too. Understanding the worst thing not being that bad can be a positive in the mind.

Some of my initial comfort zone challenges early on were to do with knowledge. For example, to see an estate agent I felt I needed to know more. To have that conversation with a vendor, would I be prying into their personal life too much? In borrowing from an investor, would I be exploiting them? In renting a house out, what if the tenants trash it? These can start to look a bit like the FEAR questions I've talked about above.

So I learned the top tips and examples about speaking to estate agents. I tried them out with a friend, practising them out loud and on the phone first. Afterwards, the reality was never quite so bad. Talking to vendors or potential investors, I realised that all I needed to do was ask the right questions and listen. Never to assume. In helping solve their problem I would be supporting them.

For example, we bought one property that had 'fallen through' several times – the vendor had found their dream home and needed to sell fast to secure it. In another vendor's property, there was a structural issue that we could help them understand and work through to a sale. Investors may be earning very little on their savings, so by us helping them to use the funds, they could earn much more. That way, it didn't become such a big issue in my mind, and honestly, in each of these situations, we were really helping solve the owners' or investors' issues.

CASE STUDY 3: Converting a property to a multi-let

MONTAGUE ROAD – Four-bed terraced family home converted to a six-bed HMO

Working with estate agents and building a rapport and trust with them meant that if there was a vendor keen to progress fast, the agent would call us. Our goals for returns meant that competing in the open market for houses wasn't going to achieve our return on investment.

Objective: To achieve a high monthly cash flow – return on capital invested (ROI) greater than 15%.

Strategy: Four-bed terraced houses in Portsmouth with the potential to convert to a six-bed HMO using loft space.

How did we find the property? Via an agent who knew me and I'd proved to them that we could act fast in a situation where the vendor needed to move quickly. I was in their 'little black book' as I call it – the people they call that they can trust to progress.

Position of the vendor: The vendor had two previous sales fall through due to different reasons. She had her heart set on a house in Devon, which she had already been proceeding on and was at risk of the chain breaking. Highly motivated, she was desperate to find a buyer who was going to be able to move fast and provide certainty, and as a result she was prepared to reduce the price significantly, subject to us completing by a certain date.

Funding: We had a list of investors who were interested in working with us at this stage, so we bought it with a specialist HMO mortgage and joint venture deposit funds.

Workload: The layout of this property was perfect, enabling us to have the space for six large double rooms and no need for additional ensuites. Not much structural work was needed – just redecoration, a replacement bathroom and the usual refurb needed for HMO safety requirements.

Issues: Delivering the refurbishment on time and within budget needed managing. This time, it wasn't just our money but two other partners' money as well. So we needed to communicate regularly and be accountable to them too.

Numbers:

Asking price: £258,000 (Dec 2014)
Offered: £225,000
(with condition we'd complete in six weeks)

Stamp duty	£2,250
Legal costs	£1,500
Valuation	£480
Mortgage arrangement fee	£1,800
Deposit funds	£56,250
Refurb one-off	£11,550
Total capital in	**£73,830**
(from investor)	
Monthly rental gross:	**£2,850**

Monthly operating costs:

Mortgage	£700
Council tax	£170
Utilities	£260
Broadband	£30
Insurance	£30
Agent	£365
(incl cleaning £15pw & maintenance)	
Total monthly costs	**£1,555**

Annual costs:

Gas safety	£60
Fire safety	£80
Garden	£50
TV licence	£145
HMO licence	£245
Total average pm	**£50**

Total monthly av costs   <u>£1,605</u>
Net profit per month   <u>£1245</u>
(no voids)

JV split 50:50   £622

Return on capital invested (ROI):
(£622*12)/(£73,830) = 10.1% (to our investors)

Plus points:

- As a joint venture with very little of our own money in the deal, we had this opportunity to make a return from no capital in.

- Making a monthly cash flow return and giving investors a return too is a win-win and very satisfying.

Lessons learned:

- The discipline of working with other people's money gave us more focus on the costs and communicating progress against the plan.

- We used a detailed schedule of works for the refurb to be very specific about what was required.

- Introducing investors and making sure they had the same aims was important too.

- We needed detailed agreements in writing to make sure that all of us were clear on the relationships within the joint venture, and our shared responsibilities for different risks and scenarios.

Current situation: There have been times when additional maintenance, problems with bathrooms and a few tenants not paying have reduced the profit significantly, so the returns have been lower than our expectations at times.

HMOs do need to continue to be managed well, and if you are outsourcing to an agent you must make sure they are proactive.

3.4 What Happens When Things Go Wrong?

If you've done enough learning and got the support in place, then the impacts of things going wrong will be minimised. In our property experience, there are some things that can happen no matter how much you prepare. Here are some examples:

Property defects: Pretty basic advice, but if I were to ask you whether you had a buildings survey for the home you bought, the answer would have been a resounding "Yes." The key areas that can cause big financial problems are structural issues such as subsidence, the roof, drains, damp and floors, etc. Many things are not visible when viewing a property and can easily be hidden behind decoration or fixtures and fittings.

We've had two properties where major problems were found and we ended up renegotiating the offer based on the facts gleaned from the survey. In one case, they rejected the second offer, but armed with the facts it gives you a really good negotiating position.

Top tips: It's advisable to get a full structural survey once an offer has been accepted. A house survey is an assessment of a property, which identifies any major issues for a prospective buyer. House surveys are undertaken by chartered surveyors, who will visit the property, conduct an inspection and prepare a report outlining any problems they've found. It will take them a few hours to view and a few days to report, and they cost in the region of £400–£1,000 depending on the size of the building.

Always use a qualified surveyor from the Royal Institution of Chartered Surveyors (RICS). These are easily found online or via your estate agent. Compare different companies by getting a couple of quotes though, as often agents are paid a commission.

I had a checklist of things to look for when viewing a property – a clipboard of reminders when I went around a building. Things such as bay windows (notorious areas for damp-proof courses to be breached); window double glazing for blown panels; damp patches and damp smells; roof guttering for weeds and poor maintenance; floors that felt like they sloped or were 'bouncy'. Given that we tended to look for 'smelly' houses, I became pretty good at finding issues and getting them checked out before buying. But a word of caution: don't be put off buying because most things can be rectified.

Before offering on a property, take an expert around with you to view it together. This could be an expert in room layouts or even a surveyor to advise on how you might add value or create HMO rooms. We used our specialist lettings agent who we'd met at a local property network meeting. He knew a lot about HMOs and their regulations. He knew we'd be getting him to manage them, so it made sense he was involved from the start.

If you suspect there might be a structural issue, it could be useful to ask a neighbour, especially if it's an adjoining property. Most people genuinely want to share knowledge and it can lead to a lot of additional information you wouldn't necessarily get from a survey. Of course get a specialist structural engineer out too, but the neighbour can make it easier to pinpoint the true issue.

CASE STUDY 4: Be open and honest; don't trust the estate agent

FOUNDRY LANE – Semi-detached property with two flats on one freehold title

This example was early on in our first learning year after we'd bought our first HMO. This semi-detached property had been converted into two flats but was on one freehold title. We spent time considering our options on it, and because both flats were occupied, it was difficult to view it properly. However, we put an offer in to express our interest and start negotiations.

Objective: Short-term flip – buy, sort out legals and sell (Jan 2014).

Strategy: The property was one freehold house that had already been converted into two two-bed flats for rent, without splitting the titles. This meant that it was not mortgageable. Our aim was to legally split the titles into two leases and sell the flats and the freehold, thus creating some cash profit.

We needed to buy the complete property, change the tenure to one freehold with two leases – one for each flat. The flats were currently rented out.

How did we find the property? Via an estate agent who I didn't know well – one of the big high street agents with not much knowledge of property, who was keen to just get the sale fast.

Position of the vendor: An investor couple who were divorcing and needed the capital. They were fairly motivated. Tenants were in situ on six-month assured shorthold tenancy agreements with four months left.

Funding: As the property wasn't mortgageable, we would ideally need to buy with cash, so needed to find an investor. We decided a joint venture might work best: the investor funds the purchase and the refurbishment; we do all the work.

Security to investor: Deed of Trust to be assigned to the property to stipulate the financial interest in the property for the investor. Monthly rental cash flow would be accrued to contribute to the renovation expenses. Any profit or loss from the property was to be split 50/50 between us and the investor, as per the Deed of Trust.

Workload estimate: Legal work, redecoration and cosmetic only improvements such as blinds and some carpets were required.

Numbers:

Purchase costs

Agreed purchase price	£225,000
Purchase costs	£3,500
Costs of fixing tenure	£2,500

TOTAL COSTS **£231,000**

Sources of funds

Investor funds £231,000

Exit plan

Item	Expenditure	Revenue
Refurbishment	£5,000	
Sale of Flat 1		£140,000
Cost of sale of Flat 1	£3,000	
Sale of Flat 2		£140,000
Cost of sale of Flat 2	£3,000	
Net sale of freehold		£5,000
Rent received		£3,900
TOTALS	**£11,000**	**£288,900**

Net proceeds = £277,900

Capital gain = £277,900 - £231,000 = £46,900

Gross ROI = 46.9/231 = 20.3%

50% JV ROI = 10.15%

For investor:
- Funds in = £231,000
- Funds returned = £254,450

Based on these numbers, we made an offer subject to survey, which was accepted.

Issues

Damp was apparent in the front bay of the property and there seemed to be a drain issue at the rear, so we decided to call in some experts to investigate. Often, damp courses can fail for a number of reasons – garden height and subsidence being two common ones. We were aware of subsidence issues across some parts of Southampton, and this house was in one of those areas, so we wondered if that might have caused issues related to this. We enquired via the agent to the owner to ask them if they had had any investigations or work done. They said categorically no. We might have left it there and believed them... but of course we didn't.

We paid for a detailed damp survey report and a drains survey.

As a semi-detached property, if there had been problems in the past it was likely to have impacted on both properties, so I called in on the neighbour one evening. The lady was very welcoming and had so much information to share about the problem. She had had work done herself and was able to give us evidence and the name of the company that carried it out too. We very nearly bought her house as she said she was looking to sell it that year, but she had done a lot of modernisation and would have wanted too much for our aims.

The experts told us that indeed there was a real issue that needed fixing and that there was evidence of subsidence. The agent told us that was 'rubbish' and that we 'didn't know what we were doing'.

We discovered the following:

Subsidence issues were present when the current owners purchased the property in the mid-1990s.

With several areas of cracking, a survey was undertaken to assess the ongoing movement of the property. The results confirmed that:

- Foundations were shallow brick pad style and were sitting on clay and gravel subsoil. These will always be a source of movement.

- Underpinning specification generated in the 1990s but no underpinning had been performed.

- Slight movement evident since assessment in the 1990s.

- Front bay showed signs of fairly recent movement – new cracks in the ceiling since last redecoration.

Suggested course of action:

- Monitor movement/cracking over six-month period to assess if movement was still evident and what pattern of movement was occurring. If movement persisted, then the building required underpinning.

There were some issues we were aware of when we put in our original offer. However, following the disclosures forwarded to us and the survey we instructed, I compiled the following list of problems that needed to be rectified to bring it up to the standard we would require (those in grey indicate the problems we were aware of at the time of our original offer).

Catalogue of Issues

Issue	Implication	Resolution	Comment
Two dwellings on a single title	Difficult to get a mortgage as most lenders will not lend against more than one dwelling on a title	Create legal leaseholds for each flat, separate from the freehold	
No planning permission received for split of house into two flats	Planning irregularity, which leads to legal risks	Property has been split for >4 years so a certificate of normalisation is needed	Checked with Southampton planning office
Building Control re. split to separate flats	If building regulations were not signed off at the time of splitting the property into flats, then the owner has liability if anything goes wrong (e.g. a fire that spreads from one dwelling to the other)	Normalising this will require current building regulations to be applied, including fire and sound-proofing of walls around the stairs and ceilings/floor	We have been explicitly refused permission to obtain building regs information from Southampton council; therefore, we have to assume that work was not carried out to the then current standards, thus invalidating insurance

Subsidence at the property	Detailed survey report was shared		
Cavity wall integrity	Whilst some wall ties were replaced in the 1990s, this was not comprehensive, with probability that wall ties in other areas now need replacing	Wall tie survey required to assess complete situation and plan of remedial action if necessary	
Rising damp – walls	Damp-proof course is broken in many places, leading to rising damp in ground floor flat, which will need to be treated before significant damage results	Quote received for rectification – requires stripping of plaster from walls Extensive repairs to ground floor required – including removal of kitchen units and bathroom to gain access to the walls behind	
Penetrating damp	Areas of damp found around chimney breasts, indicating breach of chimney damp-proof courses	Choice of - Rebuilding chimney stacks - Exterior cladding or facing of chimney stacks	General state of chimney stacks indicates repairs are required, so probably means rebuilding these

Ground floor flooring	Uneven flooring, indicating probable degradation of underfloor timbers due to damp from foundations or shallow underfloor cavity	Probable removal and replacing of ground floor flat flooring; depending on depth of cavity, this may require extensive work	
Structural integrity of the roof	The original slate roofing was replaced by heavier concrete tiles, which are causing the roof to splay	Additional bracing is needed in the roof space to enable the roof to support the additional load	Optional requirement
General repairs	Party wall repairs; repointing and replacement of defective flashing; chimney stack repair/removal		

The response we got from the agent was hostile to say the least. She was aggressive from the start with our questions, and whilst we weren't pulling out of the deal, we were clearly going to renegotiate our offer to account for the additional costs.

We put the details in writing, summarising as follows:

"Whilst the current owners have been happy to own the property with no mortgage, our investment strategies mean that we want to know how we can divest ourselves of the property in the future, when we

choose to. Very few properties of this size are bought without the aid of a mortgage, so we need to be able to ensure that the property will be mortgageable. With the property's history of subsidence, in the current financial climate the property will only be mortgageable if it is underpinned. So, this is not a reflection of anything that the current owners did or did not do in the 1990s, just a reflection of the current mortgage market. In our calculations for the viability of this property as an investment, we therefore need to make allowance for the cost of underpinning.

If we were to own the property, we would want to ensure that adequate fire and sound-proofing are in place to ensure that the flats are both safe and well sound-insulated. This is a personal value and again, no reflection on the current owners. However, as an investment, we would still need to account for these costs.

The other major area we see as a risk is the complete breakdown of the damp-proof course. While a chemical DPC will keep the walls dry in the living areas, they operate above the floor level, meaning that the floor timbers will be at permanent risk of rotting. The usual way to eliminate this risk is to replace the suspended floors with concrete slab flooring where the DPC can be incorporated into the slab. However, with a property such as this, the addition of concrete floors will impose significant strain on the foundations and substrata, resulting in a high risk of further movement in the building. So, it is not advisable to take this course of action.

It is to mitigate against these risks that we have had to offer the price we have."

The owners were not prepared to negotiate to this extent, so we walked away from the deal, several thousand pounds lighter from the costs of the investigations but relieved we hadn't committed. We didn't worry that our relations with the agent were poor – we'd kept to our values of open, honest dealings.

Plus points:

- A motivated seller who may have been prepared to negotiate, given they were keen to resolve the divorce situation.

- A problem property that was not mortgageable, reducing the number of people who could potentially purchase.

- Structural issues giving cause for more negotiation opportunities.

Lessons learned:

- Get the experts in to check potential issues.

- Find out from neighbours information you may not glean from elsewhere.

- Spend a little bit of money now to avoid the cost of commitment later.

- Don't always trust what an agent tells you.

- Put your reasons in writing for any change to offer amount – facts are compelling and it builds trust. This agent I hadn't got to know prior to this opportunity and therefore she considered us as amateurs. She was motivated by the deal, not the negotiation. I chose not to work with them in future.

- The golden rule of always needing a cash buffer proved right in this case. We needed to be able to afford to walk away.

Current situation: Nine months later, the owners sold each flat separately, so they must have done the work themselves and split the title too. So they were not as motivated as we had hoped and I like to think we helped them understand how they could add the value themselves!

Tenants: Tenants are the lifeblood of a property professional, as they pay the bills. If you have an issue, then this can cause cash flow problems, and you do want to make sure what you provide is suitable for the tenant too. In our five years, we've had three incidents of tenants leaving and taking the furniture with them! We've had two disruptive tenants resulting in complaints from neighbours, and two cases where the tenant has left the property in a very poor state. Our managing agent does the rental chasing and arrears management, which is a regular issue of course, but this is factored into our financial calculations.

In single- or multi-let properties, the tenants will have a contract for 6 or 12 months, called an assured shorthold tenancy agreement (AST). There are specific clauses for the notice period and deposits, alongside all the rules and regulations needed. These include things such as the rent review, the energy performance certificate for the building

(EPC), gas and electrical safety certificates etc. Deposits taken must be held in a government controlled scheme.

With one of the properties we bought with tenants in situ, we suspected cannabis plants were being grown in one of the rooms. Not long after the purchase I surprised the tenant and found the handful of plants being grown in his wardrobe. After he scarpered, I called the police and they seized the evidence and his passport. Luckily there was nothing being grown elsewhere in the property, for example the attic.

> **Top tips:** Use a professional to do the reference checks, draw up the rental contracts and take the deposits. It's a minefield if you don't know what you are doing. Make sure the property is checked regularly – pre-arranged visits for a single-let property, or in a shared house maybe have a weekly cleaner for the communal areas (the agent will manage that). That way, early signs of problems can be spotted.

Get to know the tenant by showing them around the property yourself, or check your agent does this. Good HMO agents will of course look to find tenants that will get on together in a shared house and help them set house rules, for example how they manage kitchen cupboards and shelving space, putting the bins out, etc.

Agree an inventory of a property or room with the tenant. Include photographs too, so that if there is a dispute at the end of the tenancy period you have evidence.

Pay your agent a bonus for long-stay tenants, if appropriate with your strategy. When taking on existing tenants with a property purchase, always get new tenancy contracts drawn up and signed ahead of completion.

Keep an eye on the electricity bill to detect increased use of lamps for cannabis growing. For us this issue hasn't reared its head again – but the possibility has stuck with me!

Rules change: There are a lot of rules and regulations for a landlord, many of which are around standards including safety, size of rooms, facilities, tax requirements, etc. These can be national or local council led. If changes occur, you might find yourself needing to change things in your rental property that incur additional costs.

Top tips: Get the best education you can to understand current rules, and then stay aware of any changes. Get good advisors and stay involved with property networks so you can hear about changes early on. A great example of this is the tax changes introduced in April 2017, preventing landlords from offsetting mortgage interest, or any other property finance, as tax deductible. Instead, rental profit will be taxed with a maximum deduction for finance costs of 20%, the basic tax rate, by 2021.

There are always ways to pre-empt or minimise the impact. In the example of tax, the solution can often be to create a different entity like a limited company, but that's a big step and has costs associated with it. But each person is different and their own tax position needs to be taken into account. Never just assume that because other people are doing it, you should. Take proper advice from a specialist tax advisor and someone who is also very close to the property investing world.

Networking is vital, and can be fun too. We've learned about rule changes as well as met many of our power team members through attending regular monthly networks and hearing from the experts.

Maintenance: Just like with your own home, things need to be maintained, and importantly, the most expensive things such as heating, plumbing, electrical wiring, fire alarms, etc. could cause a major issue.

> **Top tips:** On the initial purchase, factor into the numbers the costs of refurbishing and getting things fixed and updated before renting the property out.

Consider taking out a boiler and plumbing insurance contract, especially if you are not replacing things as new.

Do an annual check to see what is needed. Don't always rely on the agent to do this or you could ask them to do it for a fee and provide photos of specific areas of the property.

Always use expert companies with insurance and a track record.

Use weekly cleaners to clean the communal areas of HMOs as well as gardeners to maintain hedges and grass.

This ensures that there is a regular assessment of the property and an early warning of potential problems.

Finance doesn't get approved or not in time for the purchase deadline: Whether it's a mortgage or a personal investor, there will be times when something crops up and the funding is not available. On a deal we were doing, we did have a large investor pull out because of personal reasons and we had to find someone very quickly as we were just a week away from completing! This was a big lesson to learn.

> **Top tips:** Get a mortgage approval in advance, build up a relationship with a good investor mortgage broker who knows the different lenders and which one would work best for your own personal circumstances and experiences.

Keep in touch with investors regularly, before and after they have lent to you. Ask them how often they would like to hear from you too, as they might have a different view from yours. Always have a back-up. This could be another investor or a bridging loan, just in case of need.

CASE STUDY 5:
Things can and do go wrong – estimates against budget and then rules change

SIR GEORGE'S ROAD – Semi-detached existing HMO, poorly managed

Fast running out of our own capital money, this project fulfilled one of our aims – to buy an existing HMO and do it up to the standard we wanted all our houses to become. This property was a five-bed HMO and had existing tenants who paid in cash each week to the landlord.

Objective: To achieve a high monthly cash flow – return on capital invested (ROI) greater than 15%.

Strategy: Take an existing HMO with existing tenants and refurbish it over time to a high standard, to house young professionals (including ensuites and new kitchens/bathrooms, Sky TV, weekly cleaner). There was also scope to add a sixth room.

How did we find the property? This property had been on the market with a sole agent for a few months and the price had recently been reduced. That indicated to me that the vendor was motivated and might be prepared to negotiate.

Position of the vendors: The owner had moved to another part of the UK and wasn't able to manage the property. Tenants were in situ and he used a local lady to collect the cash rental each week.

Workload: Given we were busy with other projects and still working full time at this point, we felt we could continue to benefit from the current tenants in situ. This gave us time to plan and to raise the funds to do the refurbishment. We thought we might have been able to do the refurbishment as each tenant left.

Our plan was to do very little work initially, except getting our own managing agent on board and signing up the assured shorthold tenancy agreements.

Issues: Keeping the existing tenants and getting them to sign new contracts with us proved much harder than we had thought. Trying to chase them to sign up revealed a more sinister issue that one of the tenants had been growing an illegal drug in his room. This became the solution we needed to finally get rid of the existing few tenants when we invited the police to visit!

Consequently, we needed to bring forward our refurb plan and get the property to the high standard we wanted – almost our show home example.

Refurbishing an old property is never easy and this one was no exception. Stripping back revealed rising damp and lintel issues, which took us beyond our refurb budget and timeline. But we were developing a good rapport with our builder team who did a great job with creating space for a sixth rental room by moving walls, putting in two new ensuite bathrooms, a new kitchen and another new bathroom, installing a new fire panel, and undertaking a complete redecoration. We even pinched the corridor space upstairs to make room 4 larger. That was a really big project with lots of fear factors in play. Overcoming those to see it through – using additional buffer funds – helped transform the tenant strategy for young professionals and the room rental increased significantly as well.

Numbers:

Asking price: £225,000 (April 2014)
Offer accepted: £205,000
with existing tenants in situ

Stamp duty	£2,050
(stamp duty has increased since this example)	
Legal costs	£1,160
Deposit funds	£51,250
(mortgage £153,750)	
Refurb one-off	£35,580
(estimated £20,000)	
Total capital in:	**£90,040**

Refurbishment costs were split as follows:

Professional fees	£480
Builders	£25,100
Replacement kitchen	£2,000
Carpets and furniture	£7,000
Waste removal	£1,000
Total costs	**£35,580**
Monthly rental gross:	**£3,050**

Monthly operating costs:

Mortgage	£561
Council tax	£116
Utilities	£200

Broadband	£90
Insurance	£33
White goods	£160
(rented all TVs and white goods)	
Agent	£430
(incl cleaning communal areas	
£40 pm & maintenance)	
Total monthly costs	**£1,590**

Annual costs:

Gas safety	£60
Fire safety	£80
Garden	£100
TV licence	£140
HMO licence	£245
(£490 every 2 years)	
Total average pm	**£52**
Total monthly av costs	**£1642**

Net profit pm   £3,050-1,642 = £1,408 (no voids)

Return on capital invested (ROI):
(£1,408 *12)/(£90,040) = 19%

Plus points:

- Bought at a low price and added value.

- Was able to add a sixth bedroom by reconfiguring space in a hallway.

- Two bay window bedrooms had sufficient space to add an ensuite shower bathroom.

- Great location not far from central Southampton and shops.

Lessons learned:

- Never take on existing tenants unless you've already got them to sign new contracts prior to purchase.

- Always overestimate refurb costs and timelines. Have contingency too. Just because this was our money, I think we were less rigorous about the management of the project. Both working full time, we were reliant on others to do this.

- New kitchen – we decided to use Ikea as the regional shop was nearby. We used their design service and got the builders to collect. There were lots of issues with wrong items and it was difficult to put it together. It cost more in time and effort than if we'd used a company such as Magnet.

Current situation: This HMO continues to work well in the location and for the tenant type. We have had damp problems, which we keep on top of. Recent floor size rules have meant we've taken out the sixth rear bedroom to create more communal space off the kitchen. ROI still meets our hurdle rate as rents have ticked up to cover additional costs such as licence fees and expenses.

Floorplan before the refurbishment:

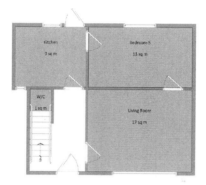

Ground Floor

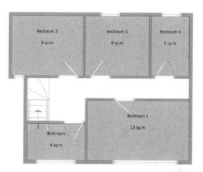

First Floor

The examples and top tips in this chapter will have given you some comfort to know that there are ways to minimise the risks when things go wrong. But I've also talked about the realism you need to know that things can and do happen, no matter how much you prepare. The important thing is not to let this stop you in your tracks. Use experts to assist, be prepared to pull out of a deal, and have a cash buffer in case of need. I know of a few people who pulled out of a purchase just on the fear factor of the HomeBuyer survey.

Be realistic and get the specific experts in to check out a potential problem. Then it won't be a 'False Expectation Appearing Real'.

CHAPTER 4:

BUILDING YOUR TEAM

STEP 4:
Work With Experts

"Great things in business are never done by one person.
They're done by a team of people."

Steve Jobs

In our first year of learning we were both working full time, so we were time poor. We had very little experience but quite a lot of life experience and business skills. So for us it was critical to work with experts both to save us time and to make up for our lack of knowledge. We pretty soon understood that it's worth paying for experts in this game to save time and give you confidence to proceed. It's also true that you don't need to know everything – there's little headspace to process it all anyway – so reliance on those that are professionals is critical.

4.1 Who is 'An Expert'?

You need to understand when to use an expert, know enough to be able to find the good ones, or if you have the skills you can be the expert in specific areas yourself.

What do I mean? Well let me give you an example. You have certain skills and these skills are valuable and worth something to others. This is why people usually work for money. We get paid for a job done and if you work out what that rate per hour is, then you can understand what your time is worth. Take into account of course paid holidays too. Once you know your hourly rate, you can work out whether it's worth you painting the house yourself, putting in the new kitchen, managing the rental documentation, etc. or paying someone else to do it for you. Don't forget that 'reason why' you set at the start. What is the purpose of all this effort? Is it to create the freedom for something else, or is it to replace your time with another job?

In the property world, these experts would be estate agents, letting agents, mortgage brokers, insurance brokers, builders, decorators, plumbers, solicitors, planners, accountants and lots more. These people are often referred to as the power team as they certainly give you the power to succeed and to make fast progress. Never use the cheapest, but build the relationship such that they are prepared to give you a good deal as you will bring them more business in the future. The property world is very small and it's easy to ask agents or other landlords you might meet who they might recommend for specific trades.

You could even work with someone else as a joint venture utilising each other's strengths and sharing the profit. A good example of this is a small development of new-build houses, where we have a joint venture with the developer and he benefits from a share of the net profit in the venture. This gives him an incentive for managing the costs and timelines.

I've always found that to get things done, I need accountability and occasional mentoring, which makes sure I deliver on my actions and have a sounding board in case of need. I'll work hard on things I enjoy doing, of course, but the other things take me much longer. If you're like me and need to be nudged to get going, then get a good coach and mentor who can provide regular accountability and support. In my property education, I had a coach and also mentoring at the key halfway point; these advisors were successful investors with experience themselves, which helped hugely. So my advice is to find someone who is successful and an expert already, perhaps investing in the same geographic area too. Check whether your values align and whether you think you'd relate to them.

A big result from my close association with an estate agent was that they approached me ahead of a property being advertised. They asked my opinion of the unusual building and what I felt it was worth. I ended up negotiating, buying it and converting it into six flats! No one else got a look-in and it transformed the first year of our investing journey. The team we used were trusted people we had met during the course of the previous two years, through the property network meetings, getting to know other investors in the area and asking who they know and trust, making sure that anyone we used had come from a referral from someone.

CASE STUDY 6:
Conversion project – estate agent relationship and using experts

WALNUT GROVE – Four-bed detached house with two partly-constructed flats

A culmination of only nine months of learning in our first year brought us an unusual project: a large house, partly converted into two flats at one end and an acre of garden to the rear. We brought in experts we'd gathered locally and put together a joint venture (JV) to buy and convert the building into six flats.

At this stage, we had very little capital of our own, but were able to bring together five private investors to fund the project and share the risk. We used experts to draw up plans, JV builders to do the conversion, and solicitors and leasehold experts to do the legal work.

This gave us huge confidence to progress with our investment, as well as happy investors who were pleased to continue to provide funds into the next project.

Objective: Add value through conversion and utilise the large rear garden for planning gain.

Strategy: The property was one freehold house, part of which had been converted into two flats but the rest of the project wasn't completed. There was a tenant in the four-bed house with a dog and a lot of things in every room – seemed to be a hoarder. It was a mess. Our aim was to convert the whole property to six flats, split the leases and sell the individual flats on a leasehold basis. We wanted to retain the freehold and the garden.

How did we find the property? We found it via an estate agent we knew well and had been working closely with. We'd bought a property through them before and so there was good trust built between us. They listened when I said I was looking for unusual properties, and this was certainly that. The owners had done very little to the property, so it had lots of original features and a huge rear garden.

Position of the vendor: It was owned by two elderly brothers who had lived in the property as children and rented it out once they inherited it. Often abroad, the main contact was hard to communicate with, but between the agent and us we persevered. The vendor wasn't particularly motivated, so having started the negotiation with an offer, we were able to have a lot of time to plan our strategy and exit plan.

Funding: The property wasn't mortgageable, given its part conversion under one freehold. We would ideally need to buy with cash, so needed to find investors. We decided on a JV because the shared risk was going to be helpful on such a large purchase for us at the time: the investor funds the purchase and the refurbishment; we do all the work, we share the risk and rewards.

Security to investor: We created a special-purpose limited company (SPV) to ringfence the whole project, offering shareholdings to the JV partners. The profit was to be shared once all properties were sold and net profit distributed in line with shareholdings.

Workload estimate: We entered into a JV with a construction project management company, who would manage the main work and provide estimates and updates.

Estimated numbers:

Asking price: £500,000 (Sept 2014)
Offered: £350,000

Paid	£350,000
Costs of purchase	£5,000
Refurb costs estimated at	£150,000
Contingency	£20,000
	£525,000
Gross development value	£650,000
(Predicted sale prices)	
Expected profit	£125,000
(over time of 12 months)	

Actual numbers:

Refurbishment	£220,000
(higher than planned by £50,000)	
Legal and lease split fees	£20,000
Sale value realised	£750,000
(higher than planned by £100,000)	

Profit to the SPV Ltd co: **£160,000**

Plus points:

- Our relationship with the agents enabled us to secure the property without competition.

- The structure we chose gave investors an efficient method to share risks and rewards.

- JV partners enabled us to minimise costs and work with people we already knew.

- The owners were happy to have a straightforward purchase – we gave them an option of us taking control and then sharing the profit, thus avoiding the need for capital purchase funds, but as a family sale they wanted simplicity.

Lessons learned:

- With old properties there will always be additional costs that are unexpected. The contingency we used was much less than we should have estimated.

- Working with a few investors brings skills and a breadth of experience to the table. We had regular meetings and site reviews.

- Working with experts and people we knew and trusted meant that as issues arose we could work together to overcome them using their knowledge and advice.

- We'd considered going up to a second floor in the roof space, but the foundations may not have supported this. It would have taken a lot longer and added risk to the project. Again, experts knew this and saved us heartache in the future.

- Splitting a property into separate leases is a very specialised area and we consulted a leasehold specialist and a good commercial solicitor. This meant that we could make sure we structured the lease for the best freehold value whilst keeping a good long lease for the flats.

Current situation: We kept the freehold of the property and the two-bed show flat, which we still hold in our portfolio today and rents well. The property is providing good quality starter homes in Southampton. Subsequently, we sold the freehold to a specialist. This wasn't something we wanted to manage.

The garden was included in a potential development project with the neighbour as it provided road access to the rear. We'd kept in touch with them suggesting when they were ready we would be keen to buy it. So there were several opportunities to add value to this particular property.

Whilst this case study is fairly complex, it does show how we were able to use experts, from the estate agent through to the builders, legal advice, leasehold specialists and joint venture partners. This is when the lessons learned come together to create real value and satisfaction.

A great place to find local experts or get referrals to experts is at property network meetings in your area. There will be a mix of expertise in the room and people with knowledge who are happy to share. I see more and more people using social media too, but it's much harder to check people out and I often see conflicting advice when I trawl the relevant groups, so take care.

4.2 Personal Values/Drivers

What determines what drives you? Are values shaped and influenced by our paths in life or are they inherited and we don't have a huge amount of choice in these? These can be really hard questions to answer, but what I've learned is that to understand them can make a huge difference, especially when choosing experts to work with.

My childhood was pretty amazing. Not only did my parents choose me – I was adopted as a baby – but they also gave me so much love and support, encouraging me to try new things and pursue things I enjoyed. My brother, who had the same upbringing of course, chose a very different path from me. I often wonder what made the difference. We had similar values in life, but maybe some more genetically different elements.

What I believe is that my values were definitely shaped by expectations and the role models of my parents – my father in particular. A very humble, quietly confident man, he would often develop my interests by finding ways for me to learn more or take part in experiences. For example, wildlife and nature fascinated me. I joined the World Wildlife Fund at an early age, avidly reading their monthly magazines. My father encouraged and paid for me to go on their kids' residential holidays, which not only helped me to overcome my shyness at the time, but enabled me to make new friends and learn so much about nature.

Creativity, belonging, exploring, making a difference, honesty, discovery, adventure, freedom, energy, creativity, commitment, clarity, excellence, authenticity, love, fun, security, courage, etc. These are all examples of values. They are what you stand for and would not compromise on.

To find out what they might be for you, ask yourself the following questions:

- What's important to you and why?

- What does it give you?

- What do you enjoy doing?

- What frustrates you and therefore what's the flip to this?

Then put them into a priority order for you.

If you are in tune with your values, you can feel so much more fulfilled and at one with life.

My priority values include honesty, adventure, helping others, energy and commitment. When these have been to the fore I've been much happier in life; when jobs I've done clearly didn't resonate then I've been very unhappy. It's easy to look back and understand why. It also helps when you get to understand other people's values and how they differ from yours.

I use values when I'm looking for advisors, investors, power teams, etc. It's important to me that the person or company aligns to my values. An example is in working with estate agents. Now this is a hard one as sometimes you have to work with people you wouldn't usually choose to, but when one agent seems to gel with you and you get on really well, that's often because you have similar values. Also builders, tradesmen and insurance brokers – you can shop around and you can choose not to use them next time. My mantra is to try to get to know them before you give them a job, or at least get a recommendation from someone else you know and trust.

If you'd like to drill down into this topic and find out more, then I recommend the book *The Restless Executive* by Jo Simpson, also mentioned in my book list in 1.4 above.

4.3 Know and Build on Your Strengths

My big lessons came from my career in banking. I was lucky enough to be chosen for their fast-track graduate scheme where I was trained up and supported over a couple of years and into my first managerial position. Many lessons taught were on leadership, people management, customer service and understanding your own strengths and weaknesses. We were put through many different models and psychometric analyses to test our leadership skills, from Myers-Briggs to Belbin, which helped me understand why people are so very different in their approach and thinking.

But the key issue I have now is that much of the focus was on improving the weaknesses, not driving the strengths. Through my property education I used a system called Wealth Dynamics, designed by Roger Hamilton, an author, educator and social entrepreneur. Running my own small business meant this approach really helped me see the variety of strengths needed across a team and why there were key tasks that I really hated, but others I loved!

There are eight profiles in the Wealth Dynamics model – here's a summary of each one. See which one resonates with you.

The Creator

The Creators just love creating! They are good at developing profitable ideas and businesses, but not so good with the day-to-day running of the business. Successful creators will delegate practically everything except the creative process itself. Examples: Walt Disney, Richard Branson.

The Mechanic

Mechanics are perfectionists who love to finish things, and might take longer to get something done, but love to pull things apart and put them back together. They want to make everything better by fine tuning things. Examples: Mark Zuckerburg, Ingvar Kamprad (Ikea founder).

The Star

It is easy to spot a Star. Obviously, you have film, music and sports stars, but high profile CEOs can also be thought of as Stars. They rely on the strength of their personality and often dominate the conversation. Examples: Oprah Winfrey, Paul Newman.

The Supporter

Supporters are great networkers and leaders with lots of energy and enthusiasm. Their greatest wealth can be achieved when they join forces with a Star, Creator, Deal Maker, or Mechanic. Examples: Steve Ballmer (Microsoft), Tony Blair, Meg Whitman.

The Deal Maker

A Deal Maker relies on connections, relationships and being able to react intuitively when opportunities present themselves. They too love networking and of course doing deals. Examples: Donald Trump, Roman Ambramovich (Chelsea Football Club owner).

The Trader

A Trader loves to be hands on and have their ear close to the ground, and they get immense satisfaction from a great deal. They are excellent at leading in a crisis. Examples: George Soros, Nelson Mandela.

The Accumulator

Incremental growth is the key to this Wealth Dynamics profile. They are excellent project managers, patient and disciplined, and work to a successful system. Examples: Warren Buffet, Benjamin Graham.

The Lord

The Lord likes to control everything. They are not the loudest in a group, but do detailed research and study to come up with decisions. They don't want attention like the Stars, and like to create wealth quietly. Examples: Angela Merkal, Lakshmi Mittal.

Here is my Wealth Dynamics profile, which in summary shows I'm a people person, happy to network and talk to a room, great at negotiating and collaborating with others and building teams:

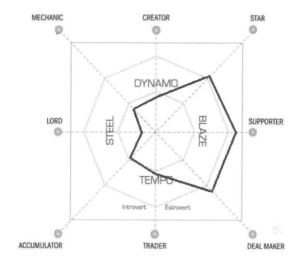

And in contrast here is my husband John's profile:

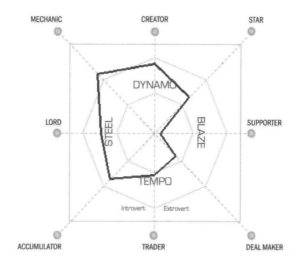

John is happier to be on his own than in a crowded room, interested in the detail and solving problems. He is more introvert too, which shows how different he is from me. This means we can work well together – much more so when we understand why each other has a different perspective on an issue.

For example, we have a problem with our IT systems and I immediately say "Who can help us sort this out?" John will say "We need to find a way to fix it," and loves the challenge that brings.

This has been vital as leaving our corporate jobs to be working full time in property meant we were suddenly actually working together, which is so different from the transactional work we'd done before. Things would really annoy me in his approach to issues and vice versa, so using Wealth Dynamics really helped us chill and realise what the norm is for each of us!

My advice now is to really understand your strengths, build on improving them, and not worry too much about your weaknesses (it's always possible to find others with the strengths to match your areas of weakness). Find a role in life that really focuses on these core strengths, then you'll be good at what you do and you'll enjoy your job too.

Try the Genius Test (https://www.geniusu.com/my-genius-test) or the full-blown Wealth Dynamics test (http://bit.ly/BVWDtest) to get a much more detailed profile of yourself.

CASE STUDY 7:
Stick to your values and persevere. Have several strategy plans in case Plan A doesn't work

KING GEORGE'S AVENUE – Three-bed detached family home on a corner plot

This example is perfect for demonstrating how we had to work with different experts, find people to help us assess the property options, and decide to wait while the vendor's onward purchase chain broke. Values, trust and support enabled us to achieve a lot from the people we worked with and establish good relationships for the future. We went on to work with the agent, the architect and the managing agent after this one.

This three-bed detached property in Southampton caught my eye in one of the estate agent's windows. I'd started to work with this agent but hadn't bought from them yet. It was a bit run down on the outside, indicating the owner wasn't too caring about the property. Maybe inside was the same – maybe I could get a below-market offer? But the best thing was it was at the end of the street on a corner plot. There was definitely space to use the garage as another room or even extend to the side to create another dwelling.

Objective: High cash flow properties with value to add.

Strategy: This house had the potential to convert to an HMO. On a corner plot, it could also provide an opportunity to extend to the side.

How did we find the property? Through an estate agent I'd been getting to know and had been training them to look for certain types of properties for me. This appeared in their agent's window and I spotted it on my weekly high street visit.

Position of the vendor: The owner had already found her dream house and was hard negotiating her purchase. We had funds lined up, and with no chain the agents were really selling us to the vendor, enabling us to offer quite a bit below the market price. We negotiated pretty well as it was easy to see that a complete redecoration was required both inside and out.

Funding: We used a standard buy-to-let mortgage with flexibility (i.e. we didn't fix the rate) in case we changed our strategy to an HMO or development. The deposit came from our own funds.

Workload: None initially – we let it as a family home while we planned our strategy.

Issues: We were reminded that one in three houses fall through and this one started to become one of those. The vendor's chain was starting to look wobbly, just as we were ready to exchange! Oh no! The person she was buying from needed more funds and threatened to pull out. She only needed £10,000 more. It was more complex than that, but we had to think long and hard about the value we could create and the returns to justify paying just a little more. We stuck by her and several months later completed at the higher price.

Plan A was to convert the house to an HMO, but our goal was six rooms and this could only just create four in the current layout. If we could add value by extending it then we could even create a larger number of rooms. As we were busy with other projects, we decided to let it out as a single let while we sought planning permission and worked out the best options.

Numbers:

Asking price: £250,000 (July 2014)
Offered: £210,000 and prepared to wait for vendor to look for another purchase
Agreed: £225,000

Single-let monthly rental income	£900
Less Costs:	
Mortgage	£480
Agent fee	£72
Maintenance (boiler repair, etc.)	£40
Insurance	£15
Net profit per month	**£293**

After the first tenant family left we changed the strategy to a four-bed short-term room rental to contractors via Airbnb. This not only increased cash flow but also gave us the flexibility for getting vacant possession once our planning came through.

Here's an option we considered to extend and convert to four flats (two one-beds and two two-beds):

Development estimate	£120,000
Cost of finance	£27,000
Development contingency	£30,000
Cost total	**£177,000**
Sale revenue	£470,000
Sale costs	£9,650
Less cost of original purchase	
Gross profit estimate	**£68,000**

Plus points:

- Corner plot – potential to add value and access from another road if the garden was sufficiently large enough.

- Detached with garage – potential space to extend.

- Owner motivated to sell and we built rapport by being prepared to wait and to support her in her onward purchase. This links to my earlier point about sharing core values.

- The independent high street agent was getting to know and trust us. They reflected our values too.

Lessons learned:

- Plot size not big enough for our plans and budget.

- Lack of experience at this early stage of our learning.

- As long as there was rental demand for Plans B and C, then cash flow could be made. Given our aim for ROI of 15%, this property couldn't achieve that.

- Perseverance – sticking to our values and our knowledge, and working to our strengths.

Current situation: Three years later we sold the property to a developer for £250,000, who did eventually get permission to extend it and create a second dwelling. So we made a profit on the sale too.

Being time poor in the first couple of years meant we really didn't have much choice but to choose people to manage our properties. In fact, we were very clear from the start that we didn't want to create another job by getting too closely involved with the management side. The legislation and rules of tenancy agreements were enough for me to find a specialist, and as we were really focused on HMOs with multiple tenants in each property, this would have been a huge undertaking. Don't get me started on the other issues we would need to manage, such as blocked toilets, problems with the wi-fi, tenants not paying their rent, etc. It was a 'no-brainer' in my view, and with every potential deal we analysed we'd always factor in the cost of managing agents.

To assess problems and get things fixed, we started to build up a list of experts – referred to previously as our power team. From solicitors, accountants and professionals through to furniture suppliers, damp experts and planners, we found people we trusted and resonated with. Some have become good friends and trusted partners. The one trade we struggled with was plumbers – good ones seem to be hard to find in the south! Neither of the children thought it was a job they'd relish, despite my suggestions!

Getting to know yourself better is such a great life tool anyway, and if it involves your partner too, then it can make for a fun conversation, but more importantly a huge understanding of each other and how you tick. Lifelong niggles are explained in a split second and the Wealth Dynamics reports give you strategies and ideas on how to respond to the differences. I find myself quickly analysing people I coach and encouraging them to take the test too. Great fun can be had, I assure you.

CHAPTER 5:

ESSENTIAL PILLARS

STEP 5:
Stick to the Core Rules

*"Risk is good. Not properly managing your risk
is a dangerous leap."*

Evel Knievel

How do you make sure you find great property deals? Our tendency was to be 'sold to' by the agents, and to believe what they said. "It's a great deal," or "The owner is super motivated," and we'd get excited ahead of the viewing. But with the coaching and support we had, and by doing our own due diligence from what we were learning, we did make sure we didn't become 'motivated buyers'. I'd see the situation regularly – the agent wanting to get viewings, and wanting to prove to their 'customer' vendor that they could get interest in the property. I also remember feeling under pressure too as their sales techniques kicked in.

There were several occasions when we ended up offering on a property that wasn't quite right and we regretted it later. The issue then of course is your credibility with the agent, who has a lot of pain if you pull out. In Scotland, this would cost you as the offer is 'binding' in their law. Don't forget the agents have different drivers from yours. They just want to sell the property and get their commission.

As you focus on a specific geographic area, it gets easier and quicker to assess properties you view and you can compare them. It's even easier if you've already bought one in the area.

Step back from the situation, do your numbers, and check it fits the criteria you are looking for. Even easier is to have some 'golden' never-to-be-missed rules and specifications.

Here are the five 'golden' rules that my property expert and mentor Simon Zutshi taught me. I'll share with you each one in turn, with my spin on how I've used them within my business. They really did help us stay focused and avoid chasing after something that maybe fell outside of the parameters.

5.1 Rule Number ONE: Always Buy From Motivated Sellers

This gives you an opportunity to buy below the market value and create a chance to add value.

When starting out, it's easy to think that everyone needs to sell their house fast and is motivated, but this is not generally the case. There are many reasons why someone is selling their property: moving jobs, retiring, divorce, downsizing, upsizing, probate, to be in a school catchment area, etc. Think now of the situation each seller is in and what the drivers might be for them wanting to sell. In terms of price, perhaps they want to get as much as possible for their retirement funds; they need a certain price to be able to afford their dream home; they might have debts to repay and a deadline for that, or owe money for missed mortgage payments; perhaps they haven't maintained the property and they can't afford to live there anymore. There may be an issue with the property that means it isn't possible to borrow from a mortgage lender, making it much harder to sell.

Now consider how an investor might provide a solution to some of these issues. Speed and certainty are things a seller may value more than the actual price.

Here are some real examples that we encountered. We helped someone who had been threatened with repossession because of a debt that had a charge on their home. We enabled a lady to move to her home in the country after two sales had fallen through. Another house had subsidence and the owner was in the process of divorcing, so we were able to give her the certainty of a sale and peace of mind.

So how can you find these motivated sellers?

When you're looking at property search engines such as Rightmove or Zoopla, you might spot houses that have had a price reduction or have been on the market for a long time.

Perhaps properties are on sale with multiple agents or are on for both sale and for rent. Or when a property is sold 'subject to contract' and then comes back on for sale (fallen through); believe it or not, this applies to around one in three properties in the UK!

These all show that a seller could be very motivated, and therefore you might be able to negotiate with them. The amount of the discount will depend on the situation, but in a rising market you might be happy with 20%, compared with a falling market when you might be looking for 25% or 30% below the market value to give you a safety buffer.

If you have already bought an investment property in the area, you could even consider letting other residents know you are looking to buy. Here's an example of a postcard we used to use to put through neighbours' doors – sometimes up to two streets away. You never know who might be thinking of moving and might be pleased to avoid an agent's fees if they can agree a private sale.

Dear Neighbour

We've just bought the mid-terraced house at 43 Alfred Street; we are looking to smarten it up to rent it out.

So PLEASE, if there are any problems with the contractors, let us know! We would like to minimise any disturbance.

By the way, we are looking to buy more properties in the area, therefore if you are thinking of selling or know of someone who is, please give us a ring, we could certainly help.

Thank you.

Kind regards

[Your name]

Mobile: [Your mobile number]
Email: [Your property email address]

The results from these did lead to a few phone calls, sometimes up to 12 months later, where people had filed the card away for when they might need it.

CASE STUDY 8:
Always buy from motivated sellers

POWERSCOURT ROAD – Four-bed terraced house over three floors

This is a pretty extreme case of a motivated seller. We could clearly see some issues and we were prepared to help the vendor. She had buried her head in the sand though and was set on needing to sell at the current market value. We stuck by her and solved her problem in the end.

Objective: To achieve a high monthly cash flow – return on capital invested (ROI) greater than 15%.

Strategy: Four-bed houses in Portsmouth with the potential to convert to six-bed HMOs.

How did we find the property? This property had been on the market several times and then reposted to Rightmove as a new listing. It seemed strange and when we viewed it we didn't know the agent it was listed with.

Position of the vendor: The vendor was going through a divorce and had been trying to sell the property for over a year. There was clearly an issue here. The vendor selling this had been duped by the agents into overpricing it and promising to find a seller (who may not notice the structural issues within the property). At no point was the issue pointed out to us by either the agent or the vendor.

Issues: Having viewed the property, we could see its potential, but the tell-tale signs of cracks above doorways and floors that sagged into the middle of the room led us to investigate further. Getting a structural engineer expert in, it became apparent that by taking out the walls and corridor between the sitting room and dining room on the ground floor, without a proper supporting steel, the two storeys above were not supported. Hence, they started to cause cracks and the floors started to bend.

Our due diligence also showed that the property had been on the market for some time and offers had fallen through (clearly as it was not mortgageable in its existing condition).

We worked out what it would cost to put right and then offered accordingly. We met with the vendor and the agent to explain our findings and to share the evidence. We arranged for funding to put it right so that we could then revalue it once the work had been completed. The vendor wouldn't budge from her position, being influenced by the agent who said they could find them a cash buyer.

We held our position but offered to try to help the vendor in perhaps getting her to do the work with a qualified technician before we bought it. We could see she was getting pretty desperate to sell and we held our offer on the table, communicating from time to time to remind her that our offer was a fair one and that funding was there to proceed quickly. Six months later, I was sitting in a meeting and my phone rang. It was the current agent that the property was on with who asked us if we were still interested. With only two weeks before the finance offer ran out, we of course said yes – but subject to getting vacant possession by that point.

Funding: We needed a refurbishment loan to put the problem right, and then this could be converted into a mortgage with the same company. We used private investor funds for the deposit and some of the refurbishment costs as a JV arrangement.

Workload: Specialist engineers were used to put the new steels in and to re-establish the supporting wall and hallway. This gave us the additional rooms to convert the house to an HMO.

Numbers:

Asking price: £265,000 (Feb 2015)
Offered: £227,000 (March 2015; accepted in October 2015)

Refurb costs: (Finance)	£64,000
Remortgage costs: (Mortgage £266,000)	£13,000
Total cash invested: (JV funds)	**£38,000**
Monthly rental gross:	**£3,200**
Monthly operating costs:	**£2,180**
Net profit per month (no voids)	**£1,020**

Return on capital invested (ROI):
$(£1020 * 12)/(£38,000) = 32\%$

Plus points:

- We'd done the deal at the price where the numbers worked for us.

- We were fair in our offer, given the cost of the works required.

- We stuck to our principles. We understood the vendor's position and were open and honest with her.

Lessons learned:

- Dig into why the property hadn't sold before.

- Get an expert opinion and quote for works that needed to be done.

- Get finance sorted to be ready to progress.

- Be open and honest in all dealings with agents and buyers.

- Follow up regularly and keep communication open – ideally with the vendor and offering a solution to their problem.

- There are always solutions to a problem – it's just whether you have the patience and experience to resolve it.

Current situation: Having got a licence for a six-bedroom HMO, we applied to the planners to extend it to a seventh bedroom. This will give us more comfort in case of voids or additional costs.

5.2 Rule Number TWO: Always Buy in an Area of High Rental Demand

This is purely to enable surety that if a tenant leaves, there will be a good opportunity to replace them fast at the full market rent – minimising your void period and therefore risk of being out of pocket.

Who are your tenants going to be? Students, young workers, professionals, families? Where will they want to live and what facilities might they need to have nearby? This is how you can consider where the demand might be and where you might invest.

There are other things you can use to research this. Using Rightmove or similar search engines, you can look to see how many properties are in your investing area for rent. Then using a website called SpareRoom or similar – where people advertise that they are looking to rent and landlords also advertise rooms or houses for rent – you can easily compare the demand and supply in the area.

The best way I found in the early days was to talk to local estate agents on the ground. There's usually a high street full of agents so I tried a few of them to see which ones were most helpful. Ask them what their views are as they have their ears close to the ground. Build a rapport with them and they can teach you so much about an area.

CASE STUDY 9:
Buying in a high demand area

ALDER ROAD – An existing six-bed HMO

This property we found because we decided to look at high demand areas of the city of Southampton. Avoiding the student areas where there was too much competition, we looked at where big employers were based. We chose to look at the major teaching hospital site, located right in the middle of residential areas, including a lot of ex-council properties. That meant there could be cheaper prices, but within walking distance of the employer.

Objective: To find an opportunity for a high cash-flowing HMO, meeting our threshold of 15% ROI.

Strategy: Through my learning, I had targeted three areas of Southampton based on the demand from potential tenants. This example was fairly close to the hospital and had parking too. And as it was at the end of a three terrace, there was additional scope to add value in the future.

How did we find the property? We found the area by going on to spareroom.com, as well as talking to the hospital department that is responsible for professional trainees. I'd been focusing on specific streets and set a Rightmove 'alert' to let me know when a property came up for sale, as well as leafleting the street to ask if anyone was planning on selling. This one was in the perfect spot, and was an existing HMO, but I wondered if it might then be overpriced.

I was going to struggle to get it below market value, as the agent, seeing a few serious potential investors, decided to go to sealed bids. That means that each offer had to be handed into the agent by a specific date and they would be opened together. The highest and most secure offer would be selected. We decided to bid above the asking price and provided evidence that we had funds and were able to complete fast. This was a nervous time for us and the agent really didn't help us at all. I think we did overpay a little bit, but it's always been a popular location and still has value to add four years later.

Position of the vendor: An HMO landlord who had moved away from the area. This was a rare occasion where I couldn't meet them and I was in competition with others!

Funding: Mortgage with deposit funds coming from the remortgage of our home.

Workload: No work needed initially as it was already tenanted and housed workers from the hospital nearby. Our plan was to refurb to a high standard and improve the tenant base to young professionals/doctors.

Issues: Competition to push the price up. Existing tenants.

Numbers:

Asking price: £190,000 (April 2014)
Offered: £232,000 in a sealed bid
Purchase costs:
Stamp duty   £2,320

Legals:

Land registry fee	£135
Mortgage legal fee	£124
Solicitors fee purchase conveyance	£810
Local authority search fee	£85
CHAPs fees	£42
Total legal costs	**£1,196**

Deposit	**£58,000**
Total Purchase cost	**£61,516**

Mortgage loan advance   £174,000

Monthly rental gross: **£2,700**

Monthly operating costs: **£1,260**

Net profit per month   £1,440
(no voids)

Return on capital invested (ROI):
(£1,440*12)/(£61,516) = 28%

Plus points:

- Already an operating HMO with tenants in situ; no refurb needed at this stage.

- Potential to extend to the side into the garden in the future.

- Very little effort to turn this into a cash-flowing property, as we decided not to refurbish it with tenants in situ.

Lessons learned:

- Sealed bids puts pressure on you to do the numbers. In the bid, clearly state how fast you can move, with proof of funds, etc. to give confidence in writing.

- Require tenants to sign new contracts prior to completion.

Current situation: We refurbished it a year later to bring it up to the standard of our other HMOs and to attract higher rents. This was also to minimise the need for future maintenance work.

Refurbishment:

Remove flooring, kitchen	£795
New doors/fire alarm panel	£2,286
Kitchen (Magnet)	£2,585
Carpets	£2,043
New boiler	£1,780
Redecorate	£1,625
Total costs	**£11,114**

We still have the opportunity to extend to the side when we have the time to consider the planning application and effort needed.

5.3 Rule Number THREE: Always Buy for Positive Cash Flow

Make sure that you end up making a healthy profit with contingency, so that you end up with an asset, not a liability!

The thing you must always do is work through the numbers: check out the return on investment, work out the major costs like the mortgage, agent's fees, maintenance costs, etc. and add in a contingency. That way, you know what price will work for you and the returns you will be happy with. Everyone is different and I remember well when I started that the range of returns my colleagues were happy with went from 5% to 35%. If you create a spreadsheet, you can look at different strategy options and compare different scenarios.

Numbers often scare people, and that fear can stop people from taking action. The way I help with that is to start really simply and break down the costs into the following:

- Purchase – key items such as stamp duty, legals and finance fees

- Mortgage – see a broker early to know the costs and the amount you can borrow

- Operating costs – insurance, boiler breakdown cover, service charges, broadband, gas/electricity, depending on whether you are single-letting or multi-letting (you pay utility bills and council tax)

Then look at the rental income, assuming some void periods during the year. There should be a profit each month and enough to meet the goal you set. For example, a return on the money you are putting in is what I call the return on capital invested or ROI – as you have seen from the case studies provided. This can be calculated by dividing the net annual profit by the amount of money invested (deposit, stamp duty, fees, refurb, etc.). I started at 10% and moved up to 20% as I learned different strategies. Now that's a lot more than I'd get by leaving the money in the bank!

CASE STUDY 10:
Always buy for positive cash flow

UPPER BROOK STREET – Two-bed maisonette

This example was used in Chapter 1. It's a great example here because at this stage of our journey we had very little knowledge. But the simple thing with this one is as a single let, most of the bills are paid by the tenant. So it's pretty easy to see how the cash flow can be made – just beware of the void periods if you don't adhere to rule number TWO!

Objective: Get a higher return on our savings with potential capital growth in the long term.

Strategy: Single-let flat in the city centre, with two bedrooms.

How did we find the property? High street estate agent.

Numbers:

Asking price: £225,000 (Sept 2013)
Offered: £215,000

Monthly rental gross:	**£1,050**
Monthly operating costs:	
Mortgage	£507

Insurance	£12
Agent	£95
Total monthly av costs	**£614**
Net profit per month	**£436**

(no voids)

Assume a two-month void each year and a refurb cost of £2,500:

Then the annual income drops from £5,200 to only £1,860

Return on investment (ROI): (£436*10)-2500/ (£60,072) = 3% (was 9%)

Plus points:

- The location of this property is right in the city centre, close to shops and the station, so it is a sought-after area with high demand (rule TWO).

- The fast trains to London at peak times take less than an hour.

- Two bedrooms makes it attractive to rent.

- We have a good managing agent who makes sure when someone gives notice that they are replaced quickly – because this impacts on their income too.

Lessons learned:

- Use contingency in your calculations of net profit.

- Assume voids for when tenants leave.

- Assume costs of some refurbishment when tenants leave.

Current situation: Next to no voids, except when we redecorated a second time. At some point we will need to upgrade the bathroom and kitchen to keep it modern and to increase the monthly rental rate.

5.4 Rule Number FOUR: Invest for the Long Term – Buy and Hold

Some people are happy about buying, doing up and selling (also known as a 'flip') but to me this is a risky strategy – let me explain why.

Understand the market you are in – what's happening to the economy and the property prices both nationally and locally? There will always be short-term fluctuations in the marketplace so if you have to sell quickly you will be at the mercy of these. Don't get me wrong, there's always some value in buying, doing up and generally improving a property. However, if you are looking for cash flow, you can always remortgage the property to take funds out.

There can be a lot of stress in flipping properties, with finance, capital outlay in refurbishing, legal and selling fees, capital gains, etc. If you can't sell for the right price, you will be out of pocket and can't necessarily move on to the next purchase, so that reinforces this important rule.

CASE STUDY 11:
Always aim to buy for the long term and hold

UPPER BROOK STREET & ALDER ROAD

An example I like to share is the property I bought early on in my learning and the example shared above. It's the two-bed flat in Winchester city centre, above a shop. This doesn't reach the best return on investment but it's always rented as the location is fantastic. The voids are low and its value is increasing as this city has been in high demand with people escaping from London. There's a good return and capital growth. We haven't spent any significant money improving the interior, and if we did, maybe we'd get a little more for it. By keeping it longer we believe we will achieve much more in capital growth than getting a small uplift in the short term by selling it. If I'd done it up to sell it, I might have made £20K profit versus the capital growth of £50K in just four years... and growing.

Alder Road is another example, as we probably paid over the odds for the property given it was a sealed bid situation (there were a few very interested buyers so the agent asks for an offer in a sealed envelope by a certain date; that offer is binding and generally the highest wins). But buying for the long term gives us options to add value and to potentially extend the property to the side. The house is an end of terrace on a corner plot with a garden to the side, so we factored in a small increase to the bid price to give us an advantage. We also made sure that the agent knew we could act fast and provided proof of funds in our bid.

That's an important factor for the vendor as there's a risk in accepting a higher offer that the bidder can't proceed further down the chain.

Whilst mentioning this, a sealed bid can seem a bit like an auction. But let me explain why I wouldn't spend my time looking at auction properties. If a property is up for auction, it has a guide price (usually well below the market value) to attract interest. In the auction room, the vendor has agreed a reserve price, below which the sale would not proceed, but that's not visible to the public. When the gavel comes down, the bidder is obliged to pay the deposit there and then and has to complete within a certain period. They are committed at that point.

If it turns out that there is a legal problem, or structural issue, etc. there is no comeback. That's why there is a detailed legal pack available prior to the auction, an inch thick, which outlines the required due diligence in legal speak. So, it's pretty important to pay for a solicitor to review this ahead of the auction.

On the auction day, the room is full of motivated buyers, all looking for a bargain. It's that psychological advantage that can lead to people bidding the price up above what it is really worth. If you've already spent money on the due diligence and viewed it with experts, it's hard to let it go!

Ultimately buying for the long term maximises the potential capital growth, and although we did pay a little over the asking price for the Alder Road property, it had so many other plus points in our list of requirements.

5.5 Rule Number FIVE: Keep a Short-Term Cash Pot

No matter what due diligence you do, things can go wrong. In an emergency, e.g. boiler breakdown or a damp problem, you need to have something to fall back on – a cash buffer for contingency.

Assume there will be void periods when you have an empty house or room, or perhaps increased interest rates on mortgages and maybe tax changes, so make sure you can afford these if needed.

In my experience, it's so easy to overspend, especially on a refurbishment, because you are relying on so many things to come good. Make sure you budget and allow for extras just in case, otherwise you'll be eating into your cash reserves.

A good example is a property we bought, which the owner said had regular boiler service checks, so we assumed the boiler wouldn't need to be replaced for a while. Within just a few months, it had broken down and we had to replace it fast because there was a family living there. These things always come when you least expect them. It's often worth considering a boiler insurance package that is paid monthly for this type of issue and for peace of mind.

CASE STUDY 12:
Keep a cash buffer just in case of need

ALDER ROAD BOILER – Six-bed HMO

I have a lot of examples where we needed to eat into contingency funds because of things going wrong or estimates of time or money being exceeded. But this example is a simple one and that's the boiler at the Alder Road property (see Case Study 9).

If something goes wrong with a boiler, then tenants won't have hot water or heating. In the middle of winter that's pretty serious. In this case we'd seen the small fairly modern-looking boiler in the kitchen and had assumed it would last at least a couple of years. Many of our previous properties had floor-standing old-fashioned ones, which we were very wary of. With other priorities in this house to refurbish it for professionals, we skipped the boiler and didn't take out any insurance either. After all, we felt we'd overpaid a little for it and our budget was tight. Lesson learned when one day we had the dreaded call – not only was it a Sunday but a bank holiday too. We paid heavily for the work to be carried out and if we didn't have the buffer fund we'd have struggled to get it done without using a credit card!

MONTAGUE ROAD BATHROOM AND RENT ARREARS – Six-bed HMO

We had a new bathroom as part of the refurbishment which hadn't been fitted properly. Water had been leaking out of pipes under the bath/shower and the first we knew about it was that the ceiling below started to drip into the hallway! Oh dear – that was an expensive repair – but luckily this HMO had several bathrooms so tenants could use the other ones while the work was done.

Bathrooms do seem to be an issue for us – it's hard for us to test that the plumber is good, even if they've been recommended. We used to stick with our team, but the skilled plumbers seemed to be in high demand and often left. The ones we used for this specific job ended up going bust and so clearly cut corners that weren't visible immediately.

Finally, in the same property, we've had two tenants in three years in rent arrears. We started procedures to evict them, and in protest they decided to take all the furniture, fixtures and fittings with them when they finally left, including the TV screwed to the wall, light fittings, everything! That was annoying, but thankfully professional tenants on the whole are fine as they have money and are generally out at work all week.

So five simple rules:

1. Always buy from motivated sellers

2. Always buy in an area of high rental demand

3. Always buy for positive cash flow

4. Invest for the long term – buy and hold

5. Make sure you keep a short-term cash pot

Five things that, if you test your potential deals against them, you can make a confident decision to proceed or not.

Did we ever buy outside the parameters?

Rule ONE – finding motivated sellers. We didn't always achieve this. But that's OK as long as you are not paying more than the value of the property or if you can see an opportunity to add value that isn't already assumed in the price, for example the chance to create an additional bedroom, add a loft room or a single-storey extension. All these things won't need planning permission.

If you think about if you were selling your home, you'd pick the agent who values it at a high price and says confidently that it's worth £X,000 (more than it's really worth, you think). They want your business as a sole agent and it's competitive on the high street. After a few weeks when there's been just a few viewings the agent will encourage you to drop the price. Maybe you've found the dream home you wanted to move to and need to get the sale chain moving. Now you can see how at this point you would be much more motivated.

For some properties, we'd keep a follow-up file, and revisit it online to see if the property had sold or not. Eventually the vendor would become motivated. There were many examples where online it said sold subject to contract, and later it would be back on for sale. As I've said previously, around one in three properties fall through in this way, so you can be waiting in the wings to step in at the price you feel is fair (having made sure of your numbers – rule THREE).

Rule TWO – buying in an area of high rental demand. We were lucky with our first purchase as we really didn't know what we were doing. We had looked at some pretty awful areas and quite a long way from the transport networks. It was only when we put ourselves into the shoes of the tenants and walked the streets that we started to focus on just a few small areas.

Rule THREE – buying for positive cash flow. There were a few occasions when we loved a property and became motivated buyers, considering prices that wouldn't have achieved the returns we needed. The numbers have to work, otherwise there is no point. The key here is to have a spreadsheet so you can start to get familiar with the variables and to understand different scenarios. We practised on many 'possible' properties and knew what price might work to achieve the return on investment we wanted. In some cases that meant offering well below the asking price – which should only be done if there is good rationale.

Rule FOUR – buying for the long term. We did have properties such as King George's Avenue where we couldn't make the planned strategy work and therefore it made sense to divest ourselves. It was very hard I remember because I loved the location and knew that we were making some profit. As long as the aims are right and we weren't trying to just buy, refurb and sell, taking the risk of the prevailing market.

Finally rule FIVE – having a cash buffer. This was essential to us, as we've proved time and time again. Having liquid cash or credit in case of need takes the pressure off. We did of course struggle when we had several projects on at the same time. Then we sought investor finance at a low rate to support us through the period.

The biggest risks can be managed if you are aware of these rules and set your own parameters. Always assess each deal against them and it will help with your decision making and negotiation. The more experience you have, the more practice you get until it's almost automatic.

As we were looking to add value by creating houses of multiple occupation, the floor plans were vital. The properties needed to have two reception rooms and possibly a loft extension to get the sixth room we required as a minimum. As we got to know certain streets and types of properties, it was great to spot and target a street where we pretty much knew what the layout would be. Victorian terraces were perfect.

Never get carried away with the need to secure the property. Try hard not to 'fall in love' with a property. You're not going to be living there after all. If it doesn't work, consider it, look at what might enable it to work and then move on to the next opportunity. There are plenty out there. The more potential deals you research and review, the more likely you'll find the one that will work.

CHAPTER 6:

INTERIOR DESIGN

Building on Your Success

"Celebrate each accomplishment on your way to reaching your goal. Each challenge conquered whether large or small is a positive step to greatness."

Robert Cheeke

In the first five chapters, I've covered the steps that have played a part in our success in property investing.

STEP ONE   Learn and plan

STEP TWO   Take action

STEP THREE   Overcome issues

STEP FOUR   Work with experts

STEP FIVE   Stick to the core rules

These five steps give you confidence and are crucial in minimising the risks of investing. Much of this depends on your appetite for risk, of course, but you can use all of this information to get started and to enjoy making progress. Yes, investing can be and is fun – especially if you are using experts as part of your team.

So what happens if you get these five steps right and you start to build an income?

6.1 Celebrate Small Steps

It is important to have dreams as your motivator, as I talked about in Chapter 1, but don't wait until you've achieved your Year 1 goal before treating yourself. There are a lot of things you can do to celebrate success, and they don't have to cost any money at all!

Write down the things you love to do – it could be a walk in your favourite park, taking a friend's dog out, a walk along the seashore, visiting an art gallery or taking the children out somewhere you don't go to often. Whatever it is, it needs to be special and something to look forward to.

If you're like me and work continuously without a break, then get so tired you're not effective anymore, that's not a good thing. When I was learning property investing I was also working full time and had responsibilities at home. Towards the end of that first year, my coach told me to go on holiday. He was right to say this, as we both needed a break to put things into perspective and be able to return refreshed. We decided to go back to a very special place in Cape Town, South Africa, where we were married. It was a real treat for us, and there was only an hour's time difference, so if needed we could check into the real world. I think we slept for the first two days, recovering from the intense effort over the previous six months. It was such a good thing to do, despite the fact that I was initially against it!

Then, as you start to achieve your goals, you can plan for the dreams. It took us two years before we were both able to give up our corporate jobs and a further year before we could actually plan our dream list and start to live our 'reasons why'.

I have to admit it wasn't easy working together with my husband. It's sometimes hard to switch off from being a business partner to a life partner. We have to agree that we don't talk about work in non-work time, but if there's something that's urgent and important, like an investor pulling out or a valuation that isn't quite what we expected, then it's hard. As a result, planning our life beyond the hard bit makes it much more fun and helps us to remember our 'reasons why'.

Our aim was always to find experts to manage our properties so that we created the freedom to do other things, and the ultimate test of whether that was working came when John signed up for an amazing adventure. He'd always been keen on sailing but never had the time to pursue it, and as I mentioned in Chapter 1, he wanted to cross an ocean.

What an exciting moment when we met the partner of our agent in Portsmouth who had just returned from the leg around Australia on the Clipper Round the World yacht race! John's eyes lit up – this was the one thing he'd love to do. Maybe he could go and have a chat with the organisers locally. The next race wasn't for another 18 months or so anyway, so there was plenty of time to decide.

"Just go for the interview – find out more – see if they'll have you first," I said. Being accepted then made it real, and the decision of which of the eight legs to do and getting the map out was great fun. "Why not do all of it?" I jested. "What, 12 months, £50,000, all of it?" replied John. "Hmm, well why not, it's just another goal." Following an interview process, John was accepted to do the race and then the dream was getting closer to a reality. He also had to sign a contract and commit; now that stayed on his desk for several weeks while we thought hard about what might be possible.

6.2 Passive Income – Is That Really Possible?

Achieving this type of dream, particularly over a whole year, clearly needed the property business to be hands-off. We already had good agents in place managing all of our HMOs and single-let rentals. However, by then we'd also grown our portfolio to include a couple of large guest houses as well, and there was a huge amount of admin to contend with. Renting our home on a single-let basis also meant having someone local on hand to manage the tenants and deal with any issues.

Our PA/book-keeper Vanessa, who lives in our village, stepped up and became a much bigger part of the business, and gave us huge confidence to progress with our plans. Our main issues were going to be maintaining regular communication, finding good high-speed internet, and managing time zones.

Passive income, also known as residual income, is income that comes into your bank account whether you are there or not, whether you are asleep or awake, in the country or abroad. Property rental income can be like that, but only once all the effort has gone into finding the right place, renovating it and getting the right people lined up to take the workload off you. You make all the effort upfront, for a monthly income thereafter. Sounds simple, doesn't it!

Right from the start of our learning, we were clear that we didn't want to be replacing our new-found time with another job managing the rental properties. Our skills and learning were aimed at trying to create the best return on investment we could, finding great deals and getting the best people we could to do the tenant finding and management. It's so tempting to start off managing a single let for example, because it's not that hard and you save the 10-15% that the agent earns. But I'd advise against that unless you truly love the role.

My power team, as I've mentioned many times before, includes professionals such as specialist accountants, solicitors, utility bill managers, architects, planning consultants, mortgage brokers, insurance brokers, wealth planners, pension trustees and more. These are all roles that make it possible for us to work elsewhere. The only one thing we struggled with during the year we were away was getting legal documents and a mortgage signed, as frustratingly, an electronic process is still not in their repertoire. They needed ink on paper – which meant we had to find a courier in China!

I'm often asked "Yes, but what happens if…?" All I can say is I've not yet had any issue that couldn't be managed from elsewhere… so far, that is! Technology is a great asset: with good wi-fi connections, smartphones and apps, pretty much anything is possible, even if it continues to stretch your comfort zone.

By having others manage our properties we are giving away a proportion of the profit. However, we are also avoiding the risks that come with tenancy agreements, day-to-day maintenance issues, issues with non-payment or late payment of rent, lost keys, blocked sinks, etc.

Our first single buy-to-let property, Upper Brook Street, was easy because the high street agent that sold it to us could 'manage' it for us too. Simple, we thought. But while our experience of the agent was fine on the contractual side, it was poor on maintenance and checking of the property. It's not the core priority in their business after all – selling properties is.

The second property, Alfred Street, was an HMO, so we decided to use someone we'd met at a property network meeting to manage it. He had a family business based in the city and was also an investor himself. This, we felt, gave us the chance of better service levels, and at a lower percentage of the rental price in fees too.

As our portfolio grew, we came across more experienced investors with teams of their own to manage their portfolios. We've been able to build relationships with them so that they now manage our properties alongside theirs. Meeting these people and getting to know and trust other experts has been the secret to our success and has helped us to avoid the creation of another job for ourselves!

Top tip: Go to property network meetings in the area you are going to be buying in. There are usually several in any city – try out property investors network, Progressive Property and Property Hubs. Not only will you hear speakers to learn from and find like-minded people, but often find trades in the room such as plumbers and electricians, as well as investors who manage their own portfolios.

Without agents managing our properties, we would never have had the time to learn, nurture future investors, and analyse possible new deals. We joined the graduate group after our Mastermind year and continued to learn from others who were more experienced than us.

CASE STUDY 13:
Can estate agents work for you?
The 'Little Black Book'

WALNUT GROVE – A house with two flats, one freehold and a huge garden

After King George's Avenue (Case study 7), I'd built a pretty good rapport with the estate agent, because we'd stuck with the vendor, we kept our promises and we'd completed with the funds. They trusted us and could also start to understand what we were trying to do. We'd been sharing our plans with them and by now they had a pretty good idea of what we were after: motivated vendors, properties with potential issues and unusual properties.

To keep them focused and helping us, I'd pop in at least once a week to talk through the market and see if there was anything coming up on the horizon. On a Friday, occasionally I'd buy the office doughnuts as a treat – that way they'd all remember me.

It was hard for me not to smile when the senior manager at the same agency said they'd viewed a property recently and they didn't know how to value it. They asked if I would come and see it with them! Well, I didn't have the heart to tell them that I very much doubted that I could really help them, but they'd come up trumps with what I'd asked them to find me – 'something unusual and perhaps smelly'!

The agent took us around and it was hard to even get through the main front door with the boxes of clothes and items that the tenant was hoarding. There was just a narrow pathway to navigate to get from room to room and even the bathroom had clothes hanging from every possible point. Goodness, this was going to be a challenge! The two partially converted flats next door – also part of the property – were the clincher for us. If two flats could be created, then more could be done.

The negotiations began. We found out what the owner needed and how flexible he might be with price and timescales, allowing us to create the leases and save money on the legals ahead of the purchase. We had a few sleepless nights when the owner disappeared to France for a couple of months and stopped communicating, but we got there in the end with the agents really working hard for us. Needless to say, they were the agents we asked to sell the flats when it came to that stage too.

This project was one that made the property press – the *Property Investor News*.

6.3 Build in the Goals and Stretch That Comfort Zone

Although we had a good income from our portfolio after only two years, we kept reinvesting it into the next deal.

We'd built a portfolio of single lets, holiday lets and HMOs – all of course managed by agents, who were people we knew and trusted.

Now both of us had given up our corporate jobs, we decided in Year 3 to move into the world of bigger deals, using the theory that there might be less competition and just the same amount of time and effort. We looked in the commercial section of Rightmove to get a feel for what was out there and used our expert planning advisors to better understand the opportunities that might allow a commercial-to-residential conversion.

We offered to buy a pub in Southampton that was on the market with the commercial agents Savills. We did a lot of hard work to be prepared to offer on what was going to be a hard planning battle if we'd been successful. Asking to debrief with Savills after we'd lost the sealed bid process, we established a good working relationship with the agent who was happy to try to source something that would meet our needs. This resulted in an interesting deal buying a 26-bed property from a charity in Southampton city centre and venturing into the world of short-term letting. This was certainly stretching our comfort zones!

Short-term letting means many things, from a holiday let through to a hotel, and everything in between, from a one-night stay to three months or more. Room rates are agreed on a per-night basis.

I've talked about having contingency in any deal and, with the example I'm going to share, it was our initial plan to convert the property into flats. Looking at the planning use class and checking with our expert planning consultant, we realised we might be able to continue with short-term letting of the rooms while getting planning permission. Still being involved with a mentoring programme, we were able to use others as a sounding board and check our thinking and plans. That really helps with confidence when embarking on a new strategy and it also gives you some diversification, although you may not see it at the time.

What we'd found in this property was an entrée into a trading business, but one with a high potential cash flow. Not necessarily the 'passive' income I mentioned above though.

CASE STUDY 14:
Moving into more complex deals

ALMA ROAD – A 26-bed hostel owned by a charity

This wonderful large property was on three floors, including an old Victorian house and a modern extension to one side purpose built for the charity that was selling it. That meant we had a mix of 12 single rooms and 13 large family-sized rooms, quite a few shared bathrooms and a large new kitchen. There was a self-contained one-bed flat on the ground floor for a live-in manager to use and an office.

With our planning expert, we reviewed its current planning 'use class', which was the short-term letting of rooms.

Brainstorming what tenant types might be looking for a short-term stay, we mused through contractors, labourers on local city centre projects, dock workers, etc. Being in the centre of the city and with unrestricted parking, that could work. Who else needs rooms on a temporary basis, we wondered.

Financing what was nearly a million-pound deal was another big effort. We had built up a number of contacts and considering this to be a joint venture – sharing the risks – we found just three people who fitted the risk profile for this deal. They bought into the opportunity and were happy to invest and to support us in the venture. One of these used pension funds from a Self-Invested Pension Plan (SIPP).

Finding someone to manage the property during this time was going to be a challenge. But through our connections while looking for commercial properties, we'd met someone who was managing a pub and rooms within it. After getting to know him, and seeing that his rooms were always full, we decided to work together initially on our King George's Avenue property. He housed tenants from the local authority in his pub rooms, so using his connections there, we embarked on this strategy and tested out the other ideas too.

After the initial 12 months, we had achieved a remarkable feat of income and returns, and by honing this further, refurbishing and focusing more on the higher demand of local authorities, we had a model that we could then build on.

It was during this period, and once the Alma Road project was up and running, that we finally started to consider making some of our dream board adventures actually happen. After all, we didn't want to keep doing more and more deals and not enjoying our lives. Remembering the reasons why we embarked on this hard property journey, we started to plan and consider what was possible.

6.4 Follow Your Dreams

Never regret opportunities that come your way, and give them your best shot. That way, you can never look back and regret not trying. It was from that mantra that our year-long adventure began in earnest. Well, not really – a lot of thinking, planning, considering, soul searching, dreaming, wondering and worrying had to happen first!

Signing up to the Clipper Round the World yacht race during 2016 for John was a big commitment. Crossing an ocean would be an amazing feat but racing with 11 other yachts around the world is another experience altogether. If he could manage such a big adventure then maybe, just maybe, I could follow and fulfil some of my dreams too.

In our business, we'd been dealing with large property prices, mortgages, remortgages, etc. The amount of money that we needed to find for the race costs could just become another goal of ours during the course of the year. If we wanted it enough we'd try our best to get there. I knew John wasn't keen to sign on the dotted line quickly, considering the issues and problems that might arise with his being away from the business for that length of time.

But we both thrived on the challenge.

Our big goals then were to raise the funds and to plan the year. With a set departure date and training weeks, this made it easier in a way as there was an end date. No time to procrastinate. Each month we had to be a step closer and structured in our plans. Both specific and measurable goals in such a short period gave us focus. We needed to stop doing new deals, consolidate, consider what would happen to our home, and work hard to raise the funds. Not much then!

Halfway through that year, we knew we'd raised the money and John signed on the dotted line and committed to the 2017/18 race. How exciting and daunting at the same time! We told Robert and Laura that we would be renting our home out and perhaps they might like to consider doing some travel themselves too. That was fine for Robert as he was finishing university, but with Laura finishing college, she hadn't planned the next year yet. She had always wanted to learn Spanish, so she enrolled at a language school in Madrid and then went to Tenerife to see if she might work out there. We promised them both that wherever they were in the world we would fly them out to Sydney, Australia, for Christmas – the scheduled stopover for the Clipper fleet.

The great thing about property is that you can adapt your strategies depending on the circumstances. Our home could become a single-let rental property, with the mortgage lender's approvals of course. Quite a lot of refurbishment was needed to make it modern and the furniture needed to go into storage too, but effectively the house helped build the profit for our year away. We were able to use the same person to manage that property alongside the holiday let we owned next door.

While John was racing against 11 other yachts from South Africa to Australia, I volunteered at Naankuse in Windhoek, Namibia, and completed my dream board priority! What an experience – lots of hard work out in the field, looking after the rescued animals including cheetahs, walking the young baboons, feeding the meerkats and doing night poacher duty on a platform above the lion reserve! I also volunteered in the conservation group in New Zealand planting trees and cutting back pathways. What a year of travelling the world and proof to us both that the business was robust enough and our team flexible enough to make it work.

What's your big dream? Maybe you've always wanted to write that novel or climb K2, learn the guitar and record an album, or scuba dive with manta rays. Whatever it is, by leaving the rat race for property investment you'll be on the way to fulfilling your dreams.

CHAPTER 7:

EXTENSIONS

Learn New Things to Expand Your Opportunities

"The entrepreneur always searches for change, responds to it, and exploits it as an opportunity."

Peter Drucker

At some point in the property journey you need to stop and take stock. I see so many people create a burden in managing their own properties and then have no time to follow their dreams. If you've reached an income goal, and you have the freedom you were looking for, then don't hesitate. It can become a habit to continue with the next deal and the next, and forget your reason why.

If, however, you are still learning and growing, then there are always new opportunities to find and new strategies that will work for certain criteria. If you've found a niche that works, then exploit it. There's no point in changing if it works and meets your goals and risk appetite. This was the case with our Alma Road guest house, which was running well and was often full. We wondered how we might expand to find other properties in the area and continue the short-term letting model. This was when we found a vendor who fitted the criteria for a purchase lease option – something we'd been taught the previous year but never found the opportunity to implement.

7.1 Purchase Lease Options

This strategy enables you to lease (rent) a property from an owner for a fixed monthly rate over a period of years, but with an agreed price to buy it after that period. Now why would someone want to do that? Well, it provides them with a continued income and little responsibility. Take a landlord who has been managing his own property himself for many years and perhaps hasn't maintained it, or his strategy is no longer working, e.g. students have alternative choices of accommodation. He may wish to sell up as he wants to retire, but if he has no mortgage on the property, what will he do with the money? He's still likely to want a return on the funds and putting it in the bank might not give him much!

A purchase lease option (PLO) is pretty advanced; however, it has become popular because of the tax changes for landlords. As mentioned previously, these changes mean that mortgage interest will no longer be offset against profit. Portfolio landlords who may already be high rate tax payers might have to pay a lot more tax, so some are deciding to sell. Rather than incur capital gains tax or have a big equity lump sum to invest, they can still benefit from the property but not have to manage it.

Why would an investor want to do a PLO? From my point of view, I may not want to spend my capital now when there will be a cost to refurbish the property as well. If I can agree a fixed monthly rent that still gives me a decent profit each month, *and* I can guarantee the sale at a fixed price in the future (so my refurb costs are not wasted), then that's a good thing. We'd be much happier to invest in things like a new boiler, redecoration and restructuring the building than have to invest our capital on the deposit.

The main things to look out for when considering this as a strategy would be:

- Empty properties

- Run-down properties in need of maintenance

- Vendor doesn't need the funds from the sale

- Overpriced properties for sale

- Vendor has a portfolio and wants to sell more than one

- Vendor doesn't want to be involved in the day-to-day running of the property

Lease options are often complex because the estate agent won't necessarily understand or know about how this strategy works and operates. They are incentivised to just sell a property, not to negotiate a different mechanism. The skill comes in when you get to meet or speak to the owner, build trust with the agent – who can be involved too – and then take the time to find out their position and what they want or need.

There is no point in using technical terms and confusing an agent and vendor, so you would never even talk about a lease option. It might be that you ask them whether they might be interested in renting the property for a period of three to five years. In negotiating the ones we have done, we outlined in writing three different scenarios and the pros and cons of each one to them. We wouldn't even mention the monthly rent we'd be prepared to pay until we were clear which scenario might suit them.

There is much more legal work of course as there is a complex lease document, and the solicitors and parties concerned need to understand the details and clauses needed in the agreement. We make this easier by preparing and agreeing a heads of terms document with the vendor, making it clear who is responsible for things like buildings insurance and major items such as plumbing, electrics, structure, and redesigning rooms, and the termination conditions, notice period, etc.

When it works though, it's the most satisfying strategy in my opinion because all parties benefit. We keep the lines of communication going at least annually by meeting up and inviting them round to see what changes we have made. We discuss the building and any issues that might be of concern.

7.2 Guest Houses

Alma Road (Case Study 14) gave us the experience and confidence to consider other commercial properties, and we started to look at run-down or empty bed and breakfast businesses in the city centre. There were quite a few around, but finding motivated sellers was an issue as we weren't wanting to buy a going concern with the added goodwill that would bring.

Just by trawling Rightmove, I spotted a bed and breakfast that I'd seen had been sold a few months earlier. I wondered why this was back on the market. It was listed with an independent private agent, not one on the high street. So I thought I'd investigate. Over the bank holiday we met with the agent at the empty property and found out all about the situation.

The vendor had bought the property to run it, but he didn't have any experience, so after leaving it empty for a few months, he decided to put it back on the market at a much higher price. There was no justification for the high price, so we were fishing to see whether he needed the funds from the sale. The more we got to know him over several meetings, the more it was clear that a PLO could work for us all.

CASE STUDY 15:
A new strategy and way of purchasing

LINDEN GUEST HOUSE – Detached 15-bed guest house (ceased trading)

This scenario was a perfect one for negotiating a monthly lease with an option to buy it at an agreed price several years hence. That way we didn't need to find the capital, the owner received a return on his investment for no effort, and we could run it and reap the profit.

This guest house strategy plan was for contractors and short-break visits to the city, and we use an agent to manage it and he employs a live-in manager to run it.

Objective: Find and transform old or empty guest houses via use of purchase lease options.

Strategy: We targeted contractors coming to work locally in the week, and weekend breaks for concert goers or football supporters. Basic, cheap, city centre rooms with a cold breakfast available.

How did we find the property? Walking the bed and breakfast areas of the city and looking for empty or run-down businesses helped us know the streets that could work well. This property I knew was in a good location and it was being sold by a private agent via the online portal Rightmove.

Position of the vendor: The owner didn't need the funds from a sale now. He was a busy man and was happy to consider getting an income from the property with no effort.

Funding: We agreed an option fee of £1 and a monthly rent to the owner. We signed an agreement for five years with an agreed purchase price. Costs included all legal fees, insurance and some redecoration.

Workload: Time negotiating was several weeks and then several more weeks with solicitors to draw up the agreement. Planning the strategy and refurbishment could happen while the legals were being drawn up. With Alma Road already operating, we could use much the same infrastructure and systems.

Issues: Clarity of responsibilities with the owner, agent and ourselves was important, especially as this was the first PLO we had done. We had to become familiar with portals such as Booking.com, Expedia and Airbnb, and the technical interface with our booking platform. We worked out the pricing strategy to maximise occupancy, and delegated as much as possible to keep our time available for other things.

Asking price: £600,000 (May 2016)
Offered: PLO on a fixed monthly rate with an agreed purchase price in five years' time

Legal and other professional fees:	£9,000
Refurb one-off:	£5,000
Monthly rental:	£10,000–£20,000 seasonal

Monthly operating costs:

Lease fee	£3,500 fixed
Business rates	£300
Utilities	£350
Broadband	£120
Agent % turnover	varies
(incl staff, cleaning & laundry)	

Annual costs:

Insurance	£755
Gas safety	£ 60
Fire safety	£ 80
Garden	£100
TV licence	£148
Maintenance	£5,000–£7,000

Plus points:

- Limited upfront capital deployed.

- Layout already set up and furnished as a bed and breakfast.

- Our agent was already managing another property on a similar basis.

Lessons learned:

- Negotiating the PLO clauses and splitting out responsibilities.

- Regular communication with the vendor and getting to know them well is vital. This helps later when you might need to discuss things that are happening. For example, we wanted to cut back a tree in the garden and find out who owned the adjoining wall.

Current situation: This business has been running well and we have been slowly improving the rooms as the profits build up. The booking system is the same as our Alma Road property and other back office systems operate in the same way. We intend to purchase the property ahead of the five-year deadline. We have since taken on two other properties with leases aiming at the same strategy.

7.3 Pension Funds Can Become a Manageable Asset

SSAS pensions were a revelation to me. As I've mentioned in Chapter 2, SSAS stands for small self-administered scheme, and is a pension for an entrepreneur business to be able to manage their own funds and effectively be their own trustee. You can have up to 11 trustees, and there must be a qualified administrator and advisors as this field is highly regulated.

I never thought about my own corporate pension as having any worth until at least my formal retirement age of 67. Of course I knew I could access some of this earlier than that, but I wasn't thinking about having any say in its investment policies at all. In fact, with a lot reported in the press, I was concerned as to whether the fund was being managed well. But hey – a bank must know what they are doing, I thought!

As part of my property learning, a speaker shared the fact that there was a way of combining your business and pension goals in one solution and with tax advantages as well. There could be ways of using the fund to invest in certain types of property amongst other things.

I'd been borrowing on a fixed-rate loan basis from other people's pensions up until this point, and it was only after leaving my corporate job and becoming a director of our property business that I thought now's my chance to take control of my own pension fund as well. It was a lot easier than I thought it would be, and of course with my property experience I could show that I had the knowledge to take the responsibility. John is also a trustee, along with our scheme administrator. In creating the SSAS, you can bring in other pensions and assets too and combine them.

It's clearly important and essential to take independent financial advice from an expert. Everyone's tax position is different and their previous pensions might be complex or not even able to be transferred, for example most public sector pensions fall into that category. But it's worth exploring to find out as much as you can about the pros and cons for you personally.

7.4 Inspiring Others

My natural instinct is to keep improving and not to ever think that I might be someone that could inspire others or even teach them. When I completed the Mastermind year of learning, Simon invited John and me to host the property investors network meeting in Southampton. This was the very first network meet-up that we had attended two years before. Wow – he thinks I'm good enough to stand up there and host the meeting. Really?

It was with a lot of trepidation that we finally agreed and thankfully we got full training with Simon to learn the ropes. At the training we had to practise telling our story of success, where we had been prior to learning and what we had achieved up to this point. It was a great story and it really hadn't been a revelation moment to us because we were soldiering on, continuing to do deals and fund them, not realising the income we were actually achieving. Even I was impressed after I'd practised.

Standing in front of an audience of over 40 people in our first meeting was incredibly daunting, but the feedback was excellent and we both slowly realised that we were role models to others and that we could actually inspire others as well. What an amazing feeling.

What followed from this was two and a half years of hosting the monthly meeting, getting good speakers to travel down and making some great friends along the way.

We were invited to teach a small group of ten people locally in Winchester, guiding them through the Property

Mastermind Programme. How rewarding that was, and to see and support the progress being made by each person was wonderful. The salary for that year came in handy for our adventure too!

It was these experiences that led me to consider creating an online course covering the very basic steps to property investing. I'd realised that there were many people who couldn't really afford the time or the cost of the full year-long programme and that online webinar-based learning could be just what some people needed to get started. With Simon's blessing, I created the content and ran a live weekly programme with some 'pioneers' as I called them. The feedback was excellent.

I really enjoyed sharing my knowledge in this way and giving people a flexible learning programme that they could choose from and progress through at a pace that suited them. Packaging these up and adding extra content, supporting materials – including the book *Property Magic* – one-to-one coaching, and my power team of professional contacts, I created my Property Investing Foundation Programme of online learning.

It was timed so that I could have the content and website up and running before I left to go around the world. Perhaps I'd enjoy my coaching from different time zones and continue doing what I loved while travelling. An additional income and intellectual property would all add to our business too.

This has gone from strength to strength as I started to get testimonials from people who found it helpful. I particularly enjoyed the coaching element and supporting people through to their first few investments. It has been and continues to be very rewarding.

All these experiences stretched our comfort zones even further. It's one thing to attend a networking event but quite another to be stood in front to lead it! So whilst there was initial reticence – the little voice in my head saying I wasn't good enough, I didn't have the time, I'd look silly and make mistakes – after the first few it became a comfortable skill and we'd broken yet another circle in our comfort zones.

7.5 Goal Setting and Annual Reviews

Each year it's important to re-evaluate your plans, look at the existing properties in the portfolio and the numbers. Things can change, events can happen, voids do occur and costs can tick up over time without you realising, especially if you are using agents to manage the property.

Although it can be a pain, it's really important to review the income and expenses, do regular checks and make sure you are continuing to get the income and cash flow you are expecting. We found this pretty hard as we were continually reinvesting our spare funds into the next deal and improving our properties.

As a result of doing this, we did divest of one of our HMOs that we recognised wasn't going to be able to meet our hurdle rate of return. We knew the best agent to sell it with as well – the one that had an expert on HMOs and sold direct to investors at quite a premium.

Because we had grown our business in a short period of time, we had quite a lot of mortgage debt and investor borrowing – also known as gearing. It's critical to manage this and to have a plan to reduce it, not least because interest rates can increase and the economy is not in your control. We started to consider projects that created lump sum profits: developments or conversions. We had of course done this with our Walnut Grove conversion, but then used the funds to buy more property!

Now we needed to learn about the ways to do development where we could understand and manage risk. We found a great ex-Masterminder who is an expert in doing developments and he was running courses too. Off we went to pick up the basics and decide whether it was for us or not. This gave us some great tools and again expanded our comfort zone and risk appetite.

Several years on and we've got an eight-house new build project in construction and are proceeding on a commercial conversion to residential opportunity too. Through the good connections we've built, we find ourselves working with an expert developer and project manager in a joint venture. This gives us our aims of hands-off day-to-day, but still the chance to work with our strengths of finding investors and funding the deals. It's our plan to use these projects to pay down our debt and feel more comfortable with our overall gearing position.

Learning new things and continuing to expand our comfort zone has given us the ability to run with new strategies and higher risk larger projects, and gain higher returns. That's a personal choice, and isn't necessarily what most people would choose to do. It's really the combination of our skill sets between John and me. Our ability to nurture relationships with investors and build our team of experts and supporters makes this possible. Our year away travelling the world had given us a taste of what could be possible, and spurred us on to continue with our plans.

CHAPTER 8:

THE SHOW HOME

What is Your Purpose in Life?

"And then there is the most dangerous risk of all – the risk of spending your life not doing what you want on the bet you can buy yourself the freedom to do it later."

Randy Komisar

Most of our lives are spent working in a day job and sleeping. Expectations are that once you leave school or university, you will be working until you retire in your 60s! That's a scary 35% of your waking hours over a 50-year period. If you find yourself in a job that you don't enjoy and isn't fulfilling, or you find you have limited time for the things you want to do, then that is very frustrating. Most people just accept that that's the life for everyone – I certainly did.

Of course money is the common denominator in all of this, so if you can find a way to create an income that gives you more freedom – fewer hours having to work for someone else – then suddenly you have choices. If, like me, you can replace all your 'corporate' income then you get the freedom to work when you want to and when you need to.

Now that doesn't have to be doing more property work. It could be working in a field that you've yearned after, or volunteering and supporting others in need. The key thing here is to consider what it is that will be life fulfilling for you. It's part of the 'reason why' we covered in Chapter 1 and the thing that can drive your efforts to make a change.

Most people think that you've got to have a lot of money to get a buy-to-let property and that it's out of reach for them. If you can understand the sources of funds available to you, then there may be an avenue that you hadn't considered. Take our example of remortgaging our home. For many people that feels the opposite of what they've been aiming at all their lives. Paying off their own mortgage is what they want to do. But that doesn't create freedom, as your own home is in reality a liability not an asset if you're living in it. It's only by creating a true asset (another house/apartment) that you can benefit from that. The lesson in Chapter 2 showed how through taking money out of our home, we could pay for the deposit on a flat and then a multi-let property. That's true leverage to create wealth.

Of course we are not 'financially free' as we have mortgages on all our properties and a lot of responsibilities that being landlords brings. As long as we have protected the risks of that borrowing through the rental income, we follow the 'golden' rules and we have a net positive cash flow, then it works fine. It's critical to keep checking and evaluating the numbers though and keeping an eye on interest rates.

Managing the risks and overcoming issues is all part of learning, building your confidence and running your own business. It's a responsibility, but with it you get freedom. If you can get the best education you can, learn from experts and build your support network, then you can minimise the risks and enjoy the journey. For some, this is a lot of worry and you do need to have the right support from experts to feel comfortable. Part of this is also understanding your strengths and weaknesses – your Wealth Dynamics. Everyone is different and everyone has the ability to succeed. You just need to know how to work with those that can help. A coach or a mentor is very useful for this and I still use one now.

Growing in knowledge and experience can lead to expanding your horizons and diversifying your property strategies. This can give you a better spread of risk, enable you to ride any wave of change that might happen in any one area, and create profit in different ways. In business, you will never just stand still. You should always be aware of local and national economic changes that might impact your business; for example, a key employer moves away or the local planners decide to change the requirements for obtaining an HMO licence.

Looking back, it's been quite a journey! There was a lot of work in the first two years to build the capacity and income to leave the day job, then the determination to start planning our adventures, and finally leaving the UK to test it out. Yes, there have been plenty of ups and downs, lots of sleepless nights, numerous frustrations and continuing responsibilities. But as a positive person, I always remind myself of the wonderful people we've met, the relationships we've built and the team of experts we rely on every single day.

I still get goosebumps thinking about it. Now we are the examples used to inspire others: our names are mentioned when people tell others what is possible; our video is the one that gets played to inspire; we are regularly featured in expert podcasts and magazines; and we share our knowledge at property network meetings.

Now we know that we can live anywhere in the world and follow our passions of volunteering and giving back to others. We are still working and building the business, and of course travelling and teaching others too. What is our life purpose? What might we be doing in five, ten, twenty years' time? Who knows. One thing is for sure: we have choices and we have time. Property investing has given us that much.

It most definitely is possible to invest in property and achieve an income to give you time back in your life. For many, just one or two properties is enough to provide the chance to retire early or create a boost to a pension pot. Risks can be mitigated and managed through a good education and coaching, and for sure the returns are a lot higher than they would be if you left your cash in the bank.

Write down how you would use the time and freedom created from property income. What's on your dream board and what's your ultimate purpose in life?

YOUR NEXT STEP

Where to Go From Here

Now you know just a bit more about the world of property investing – the pros and cons, the trials and tribulations, but also how we've created freedom in our lives – now's your chance to start! If you would like to follow a similar path and make a difference in your life, then take action now. It's really not difficult if you learn with an expert.

Here's an introductory webinar and a special offer for you, my readers, to take part in my online programme of learning. The content includes:

- Ten webinar modules covering basics and foundation levels

- One-to-one coaching with me

- My power team list of professionals built up over more than five years

- Templates and spreadsheets to support your learning

- Simon Zutshi's book *Property Magic*

- Book recommendations

- Bonus webinars each year as new content is added or updated

Sign up to become a member for free, watch the first webinar here and get £200 off the total price of my courses: https://www.propertyinvestingfoundation.com/membership

Attend a property investors network (pin) meeting for free. Log on here: https://propertyinvestorsnetwork.co.uk/meetings/ to find the location closest to you. Book and use my code 'bronwen' to get the price reduced to zero!

You may already be an investor, but want a chance to learn some new things or maybe get some coaching or mentoring around a specific strategy. Then book a call with me through my website.

Don't put this book back on the shelf to be forgotten. Take action *now* and let me work with you to find the freedom you deserve. You don't need to do everything we've done – perhaps just one or two properties to help with the pension or to have a holiday home to visit or retire to. Just stretch your comfort zone a little. No matter how small your goals, having someone to hold your hand and support you makes it so much easier.

Book a free 30-minute consultation here: http://bit.ly/chatwithB so I can answer your questions and help you move forward. After all, what have you got to lose?

PROPERTY
INVESTING
FOUNDATION

Topics in my online programme include:

Foundation Basics

Module   1 – How to choose the right investing area and strategy

2 – How to work with estate agents

3 – How to fund a purchase

4 – How to set up your business

Foundation Intermediate

Module   5 – Refurbishments explained

6 – Multi-let strategy explained

7 – Holiday lets explained

8 – Finding investors made easy

9 – Joint venturing made easy

10 – How to assess a deal stacks

Bonus Webinar Videos

Module   11 – Pensions and how they can provide opportunity

12 – Personal flow and Wealth Dynamics

13 – Property tax introduction

14 – Mortgages made easy

Here's some feedback I've had from just a few of my clients:

"I had the pleasure of being mentored by Bronwen. She has a wealth of experience and is eager to share it with others. I love the direct and practical approach and can highly recommend her."

Claus Geissen, Mindset Coach; Angel and Property Investor

"Bronwen's foundation course was such a good, thorough guide through all of the different elements of property investing. Everything was explained so clearly and the intriguing examples along the way helped enormously. The clean and clear breakdown of the numbers was particularly useful for me and being able to ask for her help with the dreaded spreadsheet was a huge relief! I really would recommend the course to anyone looking to launch into property investing and wanting to absorb as much information as possible, without spending a fortune. This was money very well spent and gave me the confidence needed to take the next step."

Sophie Gaze, Director, Rosebourne Property

"I've worked with Bronwen on property investment related matters. Bronwen has been a great sounding board for the direction I wanted to take in my property business. It was great to talk to someone who has walked the walk. Her approachable way means that I am able to reach out to her when I require help, rather than being tied into a predetermined schedule."

Mehul Rajani, Director, Mizuho

"I was lucky enough to have Bronwen as a tutor on the Property Mastermind course in 2016/17. Bronwen was really well suited to leading this group of diverse individuals through their initial property journey and has remained close and supportive since it ended. Calm, collected and with real empathy, Bronwen can take great credit for the progress myself and others have made and continue to make on their property journey."

Trevor Wilcock, Managing Director, Aurora Property Solutions

"Bronwen leads the way but the good news is that she wants to tell people like me how to get there. Her course was excellent and gave me and my wife the initial confidence to deal in property matters. Bronwen also has a very developed network of contacts and it's good to be able to get recommendations of professionals Bronwen has dealt with."

Garry Peagam, Non-Executive Chairman, FibreCRM

"It's rare to come across a tutor that not only has the breadth of knowledge but also the depth to help people understand a topic. Bronwen has this attribute in spades. I also believe that, like all good educators, Bronwen can explain points, keeping them very simple and easy, to enable me to then go away and take action."

Dan Harding, Mentee, Mastermind Local Southampton

"Bronwen is a very knowledgeable and experienced property investor and coach. If you are looking to learn how to invest then I would speak with Bronwen – someone who is a safe pair of hands, with great values, and is passionate about helping her clients succeed."

Andy Gwynn, Director, 3degrees Social

ABOUT THE AUTHOR

Bronwen Vearncombe is a full-time property investor, coach and speaker. In just two years she and her husband replaced their corporate incomes with property rental and left their full-time jobs. Inspiring many people each year through her success, not only does she have a great property business, but she teaches others through her online learning platform established in 2017.

Previously Bronwen had become the first female Area Director in Lloyds Bank, succeeding in a man's world. Her success from 21 years in banking gave her great skills to be able to work with investors, borrow from others and be confident to use debt as a platform. Another male-dominated world of property was there to conquer and provide the freedom to explore the world.

Married with two children, Bronwen and her husband John set out to gain the freedom to follow specific adventures. John circumnavigated the globe with the Clipper Round the World yacht race, and Bronwen followed, working in the business and volunteering along the way. Travelling the world proved that they could balance business and adventure.

To find out more about her Property Investing Foundation online programme register here on the website:

www.propertyinvestingfoundation.com/membership

You can also benefit from regular tips, updates and articles by following Bronwen on her social media:

Facebook:
https://www.facebook.com/propinvfoundation/

LinkedIn:
https://www.linkedin.com/in/bronwenvearncombe/

Twitter:
https://twitter.com/bronwenv64

The Whitsundays, Northern Queensland, Australia

Volunteering in New Zealand

Panama in Central America

Working with a view in Airlie Beach, Queensland

Heli-hiking at Franz Joseph Glacier, New Zealand

Top of Table Mountain, Cape Town, South Africa

Clipper crew welcome in Sanya, Hainan Island, China

John – publicity action shot on the Clipper yacht

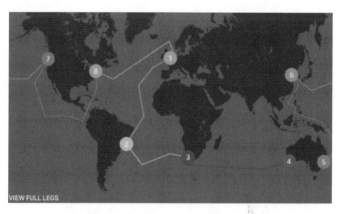

Clipper yacht race route around the world

John's pink boat sponsored by the city of Liverpool

Parade of sail in New York